ANYTHING, ANYWHERE

D1569213

Anything, Anywhere

The Future of Retail
and How to Build a Digital-First
Roadmap to Growth

Matthew Bertulli

LIONCREST
PUBLISHING

ANYTHING, ANYWHERE
The Future of Retail and How to Build a
Digital-First Roadmap to Growth

ISBN   978-1-61961-621-9 *Paperback*
       978-1-61961-620-2 *Ebook*

This book is dedicated to all the Main Street merchants of the world that are helping to evolve this thing we call commerce. In you I see my family and, like anyone, I just want my family to succeed in life.

CONTENTS

———

FOREWORD

BY HARLEY FINKELSTEIN

The world of retail is rapidly changing, and at Shopify, we see this shift happening firsthand. While our focus remains on entrepreneurs and small businesses, multimillion-dollar brands like Procter & Gamble, Unilever, and Live Nation are now using our platform to sell direct to consumers. As Main Street merchants flourish in this democratized world of retail, brands are realizing that distribution by itself is no longer an excuse to justify a profit margin.

Customers expect an exceptional experience, a knowledgeable staff, and better value, which reflect a healthy retail "food chain." Most of all, customers want to be able to buy anything, anywhere, be it at a pop-up shop, on Pinterest, or in a physical store.

Matt Bertulli understands this expectation as well as anyone. Raised in a retail family, Matt has witnessed the evolution of commerce throughout his life and uses that experience to help small and mid-sized merchants grow and scale their business with his company, Demac Media.

In addition to our shared retail background, Matt was also one of the first people I saw who thought, like I did, that the future of retail would look radically different. When I met Matt back in 2012, I saw a kindred spirit and a fellow leader who was at the forefront of the retail revolution.

Matt understands and applies the mantra that we live by at Shopify: "Make the important things easy and everything else possible." When a merchant opens a Shopify account, they get 100 percent of what they need to get their business started. The key to helping them succeed is showing them what they need at the right time. To borrow a phrase from what you're about to read, the sequence in which merchants do things is more important than what they're doing.

Some merchants come to Shopify looking for an online store, so that's what we show them first. Once they realize they need back office administration and a retail operating system, those tools are there waiting for them. Matt details his own retail operating system in these pages that will provide critical support for merchants who've gone from zero to one and want to go from one to one hundred.

Any entrepreneur sitting at that point knows that scaling a business comes with a unique set of challenges. There are shiny objects to contend with, new team members to hire, and software systems that need to be added or updated. Matt does a masterful job tackling the various challenges merchants face as they scale. He provides practical solutions that come from years of experience helping upstart retailers evolve into marketplace leaders.

One of Matt's best qualities is that he loves to share his knowledge. His company's blog is a rich, extensive treasure trove of wisdom that he and his team have acquired. He shares the attitude we have at Shopify that "content is king," and he exercises that approach with his clients. Now he's created a piece of content in this book that arrives at the perfect time for merchants trying to navigate the ever-shifting commerce landscape.

We at Shopify are excited about the changes looming on the horizon and honored to be one of the companies leading the charge into that great unknown.

I'm personally honored to have Matt and his incredible team standing alongside us, and I want to thank him for the opportunity to share my thoughts in this foreword. I will always support the free-thinking retail radicals like myself who are out there making commerce better for all.

Matt Bertulli is one of those radicals.

—HARLEY FINKELSTEIN, COO OF SHOPIFY

INTRODUCTION

Attention merchants: You are NOT going to be the next billion-dollar company like Apple or Amazon, and that's okay.

Those companies are pioneers that blazed trails we couldn't have imagined in our wildest dreams. Almost none of the shit you learn from studying these juggernauts applies to mid-sized, owner-operated merchants trying to find their way in a digital world.

We have to stop propping up these outliers as targets for the rest of us to hit. There is only one Apple and only one Amazon. You can't point to another company and say they've duplicated what those companies have done. They're peerless.

But here's the thing: I believe that smaller merchants, the ones between $1 million and $20 million in sales, add just as much value to the world as the billion-dollar ones, if not more. These companies provide well-paying, meaningful jobs to millions of people. They create significant value and often have greater social impact. It's them, not the outliers, that form the economic engine of North America, and I want to use this book to help ensure that engine stays running for a long time.

If you're one of these merchants, a big first step for you is setting objectives that are repeatable, predictable, and achievable. You can admire the Goliaths all you want, but you shouldn't emulate them. The rest of us are like David—we have to arm ourselves with slingshots and create our own rules.

My philosophy is at odds with the goal of so many entrepreneurs I talk with throughout North America who are passionate and have amazing ideas, but think they have to build the next billion-dollar business to get an exit as fast as they can. I think we need dreamers who set out to build the next Facebook, but we have to recognize that those people are incredibly rare. Most of us entrepreneurs are capable of building businesses that are meaningful and have tremendous impact without being the next billion-dollar unicorn.

As a lifelong engineer, I prefer a tactical and calculated approach that allows me to build something that's more likely to succeed. That's what I want for the next generation of entrepreneurs—to see them consistently hitting doubles instead of just swinging for the fences under the guise that failure is a good thing. But that's hard to do in a world where everyone is telling you that you've got to be the next Apple or Amazon.

So, I'm writing this book for all the little guys who've gone from zero to one with Ecommerce and now want to go from one to one hundred. I work with businesses like these every day to provide the strategy, design, and development services needed to get them operational at scale. I'm not the guy you call to get your company off the ground, but if you're already flying and want to hit new heights, you're in the right place.

At the end of this book, you'll have an Ecommerce framework we call the Commerce Canvas that you can use in your business and that will serve as your everyday operating system. We're not going to dive deep into specific tactics on things like Facebook marketing, because there are specialists who can help you in those areas. Rather, we'll look at answering questions like the following:

- ♀ What are the things you need to be doing every day, week, month, and year?
- ♀ What numbers should you be looking at as indicators of success?
- ♀ What should your team look like and what kind of technology should you use?
- ♀ How do you know when you should implement different tactics?

The beauty of the Commerce Canvas is that its relevance never fades. Just as the North Star has guided travelers for centuries, the Commerce Canvas is a roadmap that points you in the right direction and gives you the parameters you need to stay on track.

Right now, it's tough for merchants to see that North Star because of all the junk that's floating out there. I'm going to cut through the bullshit for you and deliver a playbook that has never been written until now. In these pages, you'll find a step-by-step process that will culminate in the creation of your very own Commerce Canvas. I've even assembled templates for you to use as you work your way through the book.

I get excited just thinking about it! But before we get too deep into our adventure, let me answer a couple of questions you might be wondering about:

"Who the hell are you, and why should I listen to a word you say?"

GROWING UP IN A RETAIL FAMILY

My name is Matt Bertulli, and I'm delighted you're reading this book.

I grew up in a family of retailers. We owned home decor stores in Sudbury, Ontario, that were in business for fifty years by the time the doors closed. Three generations of my family—parents, grandparents, siblings, cousins—worked in those stores. When I say I grew up in the retail world, I quite literally grew up in the backroom of a store.

Instead of staying at home with a babysitter, I spent my days watching my grandfather run his business. I was a kid when he got his first accounting system on floppy disk, but I distinctly remember watching him struggle to get that shit working on his computer. Retail software has come a long way since the days of floppy disks.

At least that's what I thought until I started Demac Media about twenty-five years later and worked with a company that was still running my grandfather's old system. You see this all the time in retail, where old-school merchants refuse to give up the systems that have worked for thirty years. While it's easy to chastise them for not getting with the times, it's also impressive that they've been around for decades in an industry where, today, lengthy tenure is rare.

I had ten years' experience developing software by the time I was university-aged, which in my mind meant I was a software engineer without the formal education. Eager to escape the retail world I'd grown up in, I chose to study software engineering. I lasted four months at Laurentian University before I accepted a job working in Sweden for a company called MGON, which essentially sold add-ons online for The Sims video games. I thought I'd escaped retail, when, in reality, I'd simply shifted to Ecommerce.

I was completely in denial, though. If you had asked me, my job was software development, damn it, not Ecommerce. I did this head-in-the-sand routine for years. Guess what my next job involved? Selling conference tickets, flights, and hotels for big corporate events for a company called Exposoft. Did I consider myself in Ecommerce at that point? Nope!

My next stop was with a company called NetSuite. I worked with manufacturers, distributors, and retailers helping them build ERP (enterprise resource planning) software solutions focused on finance, Ecommerce, logistics, and product management. That job just screams retail, doesn't it? Anybody can see that.

Not me. You could have placed a giant neon sign reading: "MATT, YOU'RE WORKING IN RETAIL," beside my desk, and I still would've told you I was never going back into retail. It wasn't until NetSuite was about to go public that I finally woke up and realized my tunnel vision had obscured the fact that I'd never left the retail world. The definition of retail is what had changed, and I'd just been too stubborn to see the connection between old-world retailing and new-age retailing (Ecommerce).

It was then that I also realized I needed to start my own company. After growing up in a brick-and-mortar retail family and working for eight years in Ecommerce, I had an undeniable passion for commerce and years of experience that I knew could benefit the modern-day merchant.

I might have been slow on the uptake, but I was finally embracing my retail roots.

HOW RETAIL HAS CHANGED IN THE PAST DECADE

I started Demac Media in 2008, and today, we mostly work with brick-and-mortar retailers that are owner-operated, but we also work with manufacturers, wholesale distributors, and pure-play Ecommerce merchants. In my view, when you sell physical products, you're a merchant. Our services started out dealing with the technology that integrated Ecommerce platforms to back-end retail and warehouse systems. With my background in software development, that's where I felt comfortable. Now, we're more interested in and better equipped for helping merchants create amazing customer experiences so we can help them grow their businesses more predictably.

Our company isn't the only one that's evolved during the past decade. We're seeing an incredible amount of disruption altering a commerce landscape that was unchanged for decades. The barriers to making, selling, and shipping products have come down. Brick-and-mortar retailers are now competing with brands that can start up and begin selling directly to customers through hundreds of online and offline sales channels within a short time frame.

A lot of longtime retailers feel like they're falling behind, and truth be told, many of them are. This used to be a world where change happened at a glacial pace. I've been at industry conferences and have seen rooms full of retailers admit to having a back-end ERP system that's forty years old. These are the people who opened new stores to grow their business because "location, location, location" was paramount to success in this industry for decades.

There's more than enough news out there discussing just how overbuilt retail is in the United States, so we know that a physical-retail-first approach to commerce is likely not the path forward.

We now live in a world where customers can buy anything, anywhere. Location means a hell of a lot less than it did ten years ago, and that's a real paradigm shift for all merchants. I watched my family business struggle with this transition, and I'm seeing my friends with retail businesses go through it now. I wrote this book because I want to help them and other merchants create and grow their Ecommerce businesses in a way that's built to last.

So many retailers I work with believe there's a route to Ecommerce growth that is both fast and profitable. I hate being the one to tell them that route probably doesn't exist. I use the word "probably" because there are always edge cases.

You can grow your Ecommerce business fast, but it's likely not going to be profitable, or you can grow it predictably (30 to 50 percent a year) and actually be profitable. Retailers ship physical products and deal with real limits on how quickly they can scale their infrastructure. Their growth is constrained by how quickly they can hire people, buy new technology, and acquire new customers (the latter being a very serious challenge for new merchants trying to scale from $1 million to $20 million).

Unless you've got a boatload of venture capital, which most companies don't, you have to be brutally honest about the kind of growth you can achieve, given your limited resources. If you understand your constraints and view them as strengths rather than limitations, you can absolutely build a meaningful Ecommerce business. It's just going to take time.

A roadmap helps make that slow, consistent, profitable growth possible.

CLARITY IS IN THE COMMERCE CANVAS

Up until now, you could find the steps needed to create an Ecommerce roadmap, but you had to wade through hundreds of blog posts and books from many industry verticals to piece together something that would work for commerce. Like I said, there's a lot of noise out there, and this playbook is meant to cut through the shit and deliver merchants an easy-to-use operating system.

What do I mean by "operating system?" We're going to look at the systems and processes retailers should prioritize. Many entrepreneurs learn these lessons as they go, so my goal is to deliver some actionable items you can apply to your business today. I believe most merchants can use the same underlying operating system and benefit from every part of this book, but, if nothing else, I know retailers will find takeaways that have the power to fundamentally change their outcomes.

Our operating system is the Commerce Canvas, a set of documents that you can use in both high-level planning and day-to-day execution. Throughout the book, we'll be using the terms "Commerce Canvas" and "roadmap" interchangeably, so you can form a connection between traditional software roadmaps and the modified version we use for commerce.

I learned about the value of a roadmap from watching software companies being very deliberate about the order in which they released new products and iterated on existing products. Every move was intentional and part of a larger plan that could be iterated on and improved after each step was complete. Roadmaps helped these companies avoid distractions, stay on track, handle setbacks appropriately, and grow in a sustainable fashion.

I know the concept of a product roadmap is foreign to some retailers, but what we're talking about is simply a framework that makes complex decisions less scary.

Growing up around merchants, I know their strengths, and I also understand their blind spots. They excel at making, selling, and shipping physical products. They understand store-to-store distribution, can handle complex logistics, and they know how to build new stores. What many retailers struggle with is entering new channels, especially digital channels, and doing so in a way that creates leverage they can use.

A lot of mistakes are made during this process, and it costs retailers time and money. Having a roadmap in place doesn't eliminate mistakes, but rather makes them far less likely and easier to understand when they do occur. As a retailer, when you can look past your ups and downs and know the next steps you should take, you stand a much better chance of building a sustainable and consistent business.

As I said, you might not build the fastest-growing operation in the world, but the probability of building a business that lasts for more than a short sprint is much higher. In a moment, we'll look at a business whose roadmap I believe is second-to-none, but it's taken us eight years to get this business into the tens of millions in online sales. However, its growth curve has been steady, with no big spikes along the way.

We understood when we created this company's roadmap

that consistent growth happens only when you recognize that the product you need to focus on the most is your business and not the physical things you sell.

Once you have that level of clarity, everything else will start falling into place.

THE FUTURE OF COMMERCE

Roadmaps should be flexible enough to survive whatever changes you throw at them, and that flexibility benefits retailers as they deal with the big changes happening in commerce.

When I talk to people about where commerce is headed, I always tell them, "The future is now. We're just iterating on it at this point." There will always be some new technology right around the corner waiting to shake up commerce, but most of the big stuff has already arrived. Sure, there's some dreamland shit like true artificial intelligence (not machine learning or deep learning), the Internet of Things, and virtual reality in the pipeline, but merchants need to let the tech industry figure this stuff out and battle-test it before we worry about how it will work in our businesses.

Merchants have bigger concerns in a world of commerce where everyone has access to the advantages—technology, people, tactics, audiences, and more—that used to be available only to large, wealthy companies. The barrier to entry has come down, which means every merchant walks, talks, looks, and acts the same. We'll examine this "Future of Sameness" in more depth in Chapter One, but the challenge for retailers is standing out when the commerce landscape is littered with look-alikes.

Commerce is increasingly being defined by the idea that consumers can buy anything they want no matter where they are. Smartphones have helped us realize a good portion of this future, but someday you'll be able to point your camera at the light fixtures in the restaurant you're eating in and order those fixtures for your home. We're not there yet, but once we figure out the supply chain, this idea of anything, anywhere will quickly become a reality.

I see three big trends enabling this idea of anything, anywhere:

- Technology is cheaper and more accessible than it's ever been, and this "democratization of technology" has fueled the future of sameness.
- There are more channels in which to sell to and service your customers than ever before, and new channels are popping up every day.
- The well-established food chain and division of labor among

manufacturers, distributors, and retailers is being cannibalized as barriers come down and more retailers are creating products to sell and ship directly to customers.

As a merchant, you need to look at these trends and tectonic shifts within the industry and realize this is the reality you're going to deal with for the foreseeable future. The question you must answer is how to best run your business for the next five to ten years, knowing where we are now and where we're headed in the future.

If you're freaked out reading this, don't worry, you're not alone.

YOUR RETAIL JOURNEY DOESN'T HAVE TO BE LONELY

Thousands of niche brands have emerged in the past half-decade that are making meaningful, high-quality goods and connecting with customers on an emotional level. A retailer might look at this explosion of new businesses and see increased competition, but behind those businesses are good, generous people who are willing to help you. I should know, since these are the people we work with every day at Demac Media.

Commerce is moving away from having fifty $100 billion businesses to a place where there are a hundred thousand

$10 million companies. Almost all the companies we work with are under $50 million in sales, which is a common watermark in retail. If your company falls under that umbrella, you've got a lot of colleagues dealing with the same shit you are.

You also have this playbook to serve as your companion. Since we're talking about an Ecommerce roadmap and a larger plan for your business, the information contained within these pages is timeless. I'm not giving you tactics for something like Facebook Commerce, which would be out-of-date before this book ever hits the shelves.

I'm far more interested in pointing out ways to consider whether your business should sell your products in some other new channel, and if you go that route, when you should make the move. In the long run, nothing will benefit you more than having the right sequence in place for your business.

THE NEW ORDER

I have two friends whose companies perfectly illustrate the new world of commerce. One friend runs a baby retailer called Snuggle Bugz, and the other runs a pet supplier. As a father and cat owner, I can attest that parents and pet owners are crazy in the best kind of way, so these guys are selling to seriously amazing target customers with high-potential lifetime value. But, however similar these companies are on paper, their journeys have led them to very different results.

The pet supplier is probably the best physical retailer I've ever seen. My friend is a master of operations at building brick-and-mortar stores. It's amazing to watch.

On the flip side, Snuggle Bugz is an Ecommerce business

first and foremost. My friend understands warehouses and logistics like nobody I've ever seen. He's brilliant.

In working with both companies over the past eight years, I've watched them buy the same technology, hire the same kinds of people, run similar systems, and have very different outcomes. The pet supplier struggled to take off in digital, whereas Snuggle Bugz comparatively lagged in opening physical stores. I had to look past the surface-level comparisons and dissect their individual situations to see if there were any lessons to be learned.

If you laid out, in no particular order, all the tactics and strategies these two companies deployed, they were seemingly identical. The difference came down to the order in which these companies deployed them. On the Ecommerce side, Snuggle Bugz had a slightly different sequence than the pet supplier and that made all the difference. The same was true of the pet supplier on the physical side.

My big takeaway from studying these guys was this: It's not what you do, but when you do it that matters most. Their stories were a study in the application of leverage to create momentum.

Most of what we now do in business, someone else has already tried. There is no more first-mover advantage. I'd argue in retail that being the first is incredibly risky for most of us, and we should let our larger, deeper-pocketed peers make those mistakes. If I'm working with a company whose results differ from another company that tried the same thing, I want to know if we missed a step or lacked the necessary leverage created from the previous step to achieve the desired results.

It's not like Snuggle Bugz and the pet supplier were incapable of moving beyond their strengths to grow in the physical and digital spaces, respectively. The individuals who run those companies are capable, smart business owners. Their issue was a roadmap that failed to generate the leverage they needed to move from one step to the next. It's like they were trying to put a roof on their new house before the frame and walls had gone up.

Snuggle Bugz is now adept at opening and building profitable stores. Despite the fact that 40 to 50 percent of the owner's business comes from Ecommerce—the industry average is 10 to 12 percent—he's opened ten stores, because he knows the value of those stores as service, sales, and customer acquisition channels. He's still investing in digital, but now he's devoting resources to the physical side, too.

On the other hand, the pet supplier had to work to improve

its Ecommerce business. This company didn't take off in digital from day one like Snuggle Bugz did. But these guys figured it out and are still kicking ass as a physical retailer.

Thankfully, this isn't the story of one company that succeeded and one that failed, but rather two companies that took different paths to their own definition of success.

GOLIATHS MUST ADAPT TO A CHANGING RETAIL WORLD

Snuggle Bugz and the pet supplier are also representative of a massive shift in the commerce landscape that has seen smaller brands (dubbed "craft brands" in Ben Zifkin's excellent book *The Rise of the Craft Brand*) taking market share from the big retailers. My friends' companies are small to mid-market retailers doing battle with billion-dollar competitors and winning. They're taking market share from these Goliaths because they're serving a small customer segment better than the big brands ever could.

The last few years in North America might be the first time ever that large consumer packaged goods (CPG) brands have lost market share. IRI (a market research company) concluded in its 2015 report that "volume sales continued to slide, and dollar sales growth was fed largely by inflationary pricing trends." IRI also found that "when looking across channels, mass merchandisers and supercenters posted sharper-than-average volume share declines."

These CPG brands aren't losing market share to each other. They're losing it to thousands of craft brands that pop up and each take a tiny nibble out of them. IRI reported that small to mid-size CPG brands—less than $5 billion in sales—gained 0.5 percent more market share in 2015 and have posted a 2.7 percent gain since 2011.

Big brands used to grapple with a handful of competitors. Now they're contending with thousands of small brands they can't even see. Is it any surprise they're struggling?

A big part of the reason craft brands have come into existence and thrived, even against billion-dollar competitors, is that the barriers to manufacturing have come down. It's just a lot easier to make stuff now than it's ever been. Sure, 3-D printing has made things easier, but we've also had the world's greatest 3-D printer for twenty-five years—China.

Also, start-ups can now run a Kickstarter campaign and get funding for their amazing ideas, because high-quality goods can be made cost-effectively. There are suddenly far fewer barriers to entry in product ideation and creation, when previously the biggest hurdle new businesses faced was being able to create the products they wanted.

For example, I'm an entrepreneur who loves mountain biking. In today's world, I could leverage my passion for mountain biking and create products that cater to my style of mountain bikers. What do the big-name companies do within this space? They manufacture mountain biking gear with the broadest possible appeal so they can capture the widest possible customer base. My mountain biking company would never be a billion-dollar conglomerate, but I could build a good business that does millions in sales, provides good jobs for tons of people, and serves my niche exceptionally well.

A great example of a company that rose to prominence by serving a small niche is The Honest Company. They tapped into a loud, loyal, and socioeconomically ideal group of moms who wanted a better-quality diaper than what the big CPGs were providing. The same thing could be said for Method and their non-toxic household cleaners.

The rise of small companies like these two is incredible. You don't make money selling soaps or diapers! But Honest and Method don't sell diapers or soaps. They sell an idea to customers desperately seeking an alternative, and have succeeded by capitalizing on advancements in manufacturing that allow them to create quality, inexpensive products.

Best of all, these companies and the people behind them are doing something they love and having a positive impact on the world. It's freaking amazing that we live in a world where doing something that is socially good and building a good business aren't mutually exclusive. The barriers to creating products are coming down, and this is the biggest thing that's happened to commerce in the last decade. As I mentioned in the introduction, there are also three primary trends impacting this world in massive, paradigm-shifting ways.

TREND 1: DEMOCRATIZATION OF TECHNOLOGY

Ten years ago, if you wanted to launch an Ecommerce company, building a website on which you could actually take orders was a seven-figure investment. Having such a massive upfront expense meant that Ecommerce was a land of big wealthy companies that could spend the money or raise the necessary capital.

Just look at all the burned-out dot-com companies of the late nineties. They spent tens of millions of dollars getting off the ground, and yet very few are left today, because the economics didn't work and the technology was big, clunky, expensive, and generally quite terrible, particularly on the customer-acquisition side. These problems no longer need to exist even though they sometimes still do in the enterprise category.

Platforms like Shopify make Ecommerce affordable for everyone. You can sell your products on their platform cost-effectively, their websites look professional, and their tools are amazing. Shopify can take your business from zero to one in a hurry.

For this book's audience—companies that are trying to get from one to one hundred—the technology you need is now also cheaper and more widely available.

When I started Demac Media in 2008, it would cost us hundreds of thousands of dollars to build a complex Ecommerce platform for a manufacturer who was going direct to the consumer. Today, that cost is about half of what it used to be, plus, you can pay monthly if you can't afford the upfront cost. Some people see it as a negative that we can't charge as much now, but I see immeasurable value in worrying less about what's behind the walls and focusing on important stuff like customer service and growing the business.

Technology is also easier to use now. As a guy who's built software for twenty years, I can tell you that in the late nineties nobody gave a shit about software usability. The demand was so insatiable that the collective attitude was, "Get it out the door and people will buy it."

We're more digitally sophisticated today, so quality has risen across the board, as software companies strive to match merchant expectations. As a merchant, you should make usability one of your top priorities. Software that works well means your people can focus less on using something and more on doing something.

I've worked with many companies that started from nothing and grew into thriving businesses in just a few years, thanks in part to new technology. One of my favorites is Tiny Devotions, a jewelry brand in Canada that sells mala beads, jewelry, and accessories built around yoga and meditation, to a global audience. Diana House, the founder, is a great entrepreneur who's built a vibrant business, but technology isn't her strength. What she does know is her product, her customer (people like her), and the tech she needs to sell to those customers. She's the perfect example of a business owner who looked at Shopify and saw a way to get her business off the ground and get it to the seven-figure mark. As her business grew, she added new systems that created leverage she could use.

Another great example of entrepreneurs who created a business and grew it into a healthy seven-figure company is Alex and Mimi Ikonn. Their brand, Luxy Hair, creates and sells high-quality clip-in hair extensions. When you browse the incredible library of content they've amassed, you understand why they've been so successful.

Luxy Hair excels at choosing the right tactics to focus on at the right time in their business evolution. They built a gigantic following on YouTube in the early days of the company and that channel still bears fruit for them.

They didn't stop at YouTube, though. They created large, meaningful followings in many social channels that were chosen to ensure the maximum amount of leverage from their content, which in turn drives their Ecommerce business forward. They recognize that technology can support their growth and they use it pragmatically.

PICK AND CHOOSE NEW TECHNOLOGY WISELY

Diana's approach demonstrates something I always caution people on when it comes to new technology: In a world with thousands of software options, you can't buy them all for your business. I bring this up because the average retailer has thirty-six different categories of software that run their company. You can see an overview of these at: mattbertulli.com/commercecategories.

While the democratization of technology empowers you with choice, the complexity inherent in a multitude of systems can destroy your efficiency. How many average retailers know what each of those thirty-six systems does, let alone how to use them all? I'll venture a wild-ass guess and say zero.

Adding software to your company is like walking up a flight of stairs, in that you should take one step at a time. Buy or rent the software, implement and test it, and make sure it's adding value to your company before you add more software.

I can't tell you how many young companies I've seen pay for fifteen different software platforms and only use two of them. The other thirteen are sitting idly by because the service only costs a few hundred bucks a month, so who cares? I like to joke that software as a service (SaaS) is effectively the new gym membership. The cost is so low that many merchants forget they're still paying for software they no longer use.

That's why the roadmap is so damn important: It tells you when your business will need certain new technologies. A roadmap keeps you from biting it all off at once.

Good retailers look at their business over the span of a

few years and ask, "Assuming our product is good, and we know how to capture and retain our customers, how do we combine technology, people, and process to enter new channels?" Their roadmap shows them the proper order for creating leverage with each new milestone or deliverable.

For those merchants who don't use a roadmap, what I'm describing might sound like a marketing calendar. Most retailers plan their calendars around big selling days like Valentine's Day, Easter, Black Friday, Cyber Monday, Christmas, Boxing Day, and so on. At the beginning of every year, merchants decide how they'll market and prepare for these big events, but that's usually where the planning stops.

A roadmap is more detailed, in that the planning stretches out over multiple years, with marketing calendars, technology, and sales channels all being mapped, so that you're always thinking about where to point your people and your money. How do you know where to direct them if you haven't thought about which systems will create the most leverage for you?

The software and technology world can feel like chasing squirrels if you let it dominate your thinking. There will always be another squirrel to chase, and there will always be another shiny object, but if you're trying to build a business that lasts, you can't afford to get distracted. Let your competitor who's six months from bankruptcy throw himself into virtual reality, while you focus on mastering the software you need to deliver kick-ass customer service and grow from there.

TREND 2: PROLIFERATION OF NEW CHANNELS

Doesn't it seem like every month there's a new channel where your customers can be found? I swear to God, sales channels these days are multiplying like rabbits.

Omni-channel is not a new idea. The concept of multiple channels in commerce has existed for the past twenty-plus years with stores, Ecommerce sites, and online marketplaces like Amazon or eBay. It wasn't until about 2010 that the number of channels began increasing exponentially. As with technology, it's tempting to think you should be everywhere your customers are because potentially, they are everywhere.

The real question with so many new channels springing up is not in how you enter them, but rather why and when. You don't need to look too far back in history to see that even the almighty Facebook has released and re-released their own iteration of Facebook Commerce a handful of times. Rushing to jump on to the latest thing is rarely the right move for the average merchant.

The channel landscape continues to grow and evolve. Twitter and Pinterest are trying their hands at Ecommerce. Jet.com, which launched in 2014 and quickly became one of the fastest-growing Ecommerce sites in the world, was bought by Walmart in August 2016. New mobile technology and widespread Internet access makes conversational commerce possible through messaging apps like WhatsApp and WeChat in China. How crazy is it that you can order a pizza or a taxi just by using a messaging app and some simple conversation?

New channels aren't just coming to your phone, though. You can buy on airplanes, in taxis, and in Ubers, through the touch screen in your car, on your Apple TV, and in pop-up shops. Instead of a handful of channels, we now have hundreds.

All these reasons and many more explain why the real challenge for retailers is deciding which channels they should enter and when to do so.

If this decision feels like an insurmountable challenge, keep it simple.

For me, every decision begins with finding out where my most valuable customers are spending time. If you've been in retail for awhile, you know that customers don't give a shit where you want them to be, whether it's your store, website, or anywhere else. They go where they want to when they want to. Part of deciding which channels to invest in is understanding where your ideal customers are and why they are there. Is it entertainment? Social? Educational? Inspirational? There are many reasons people make the decisions they do with their hard-earned money. Knowing your customer intimately is always a good investment.

A prevailing theory is that the future of physical retail will boil down to entertaining customers, as they'll want to go where the experience is best. I certainly think that's one part of it. At the end of the day, great products and even better service are still going to win you more customers than metaphorical dancing monkeys in your stores.

If you stand for everything, you stand for nothing. Trying to serve all customers means you're most likely not serving your best customers very well. Keep this truth in mind when you're considering whether to enter the latest and greatest channel, and ask yourself: Are my best customers there? If they're not, put that channel on the shelf and continue building up your existing channels.

When we begin to develop your roadmap in future chapters, you'll benefit tremendously from knowing who your customers are and which channels they are in.

COMMERCE WILL CONTINUE TO EVOLVE

The earliest form of commerce was peer-to-peer trading, back when people bartered with their neighbors—a wool hat for a gallon of milk. The next phase saw consumers buying their goods from small retailers, all those mom-and-pop stores on Main Street. North America's migration to the suburbs resulted in the birth of big-box stores and strip malls. For a few decades during this phase, retail got super anonymous. Retailers didn't care about knowing their customers, because competition was scarce. If they opened more stores, they made more money. Why make the effort when everyone's money counts the same?

As we've seen, the emergence of Ecommerce and online marketplaces have increased the need to know your customers. Some big retailers still go the lazy route, but as we move towards personalized buying experiences for every customer, these retail giants will soon have a very real choice: Adapt or die.

Customers are buying anything, anywhere now, and the future will see even more of our longstanding buying practices replaced with more efficient, convenient alternatives.

Thirty years ago, you might have been over at someone's house with a bunch of friends drinking coffee and someone would have started selling you jewelry. Isn't Facebook the modern-day equivalent of the jewelry party? You hang out virtually with a bunch of friends, chit-chatting about this and that, only for someone to start trying to sell you something. (Nowadays it's probably Zija health products.)

We've been here all along. Technology has just allowed merchants to interrupt our increasingly busy lives in ways that were previously unimaginable.

It's scary for you as a merchant to look at these channels multiplying like rabbits and wonder how the hell you're supposed to be in all those places at once. My advice is to find the channel with more of your best, most valuable customers than any other and place your focus there. You need to be in the right channels, not every channel, to serve your customers well.

TREND 3: CANNIBALIZATION OF THE FOOD CHAIN

With lower barriers to manufacturing and technology, plus the proliferation of new sales channels, the clearly defined food chain that existed among manufacturers, distributors, and retailers is beginning to erode. It used to be that manufacturers created products and sold them in bulk quantities to wholesalers, who turned around and sold those products to retailers in quantities that retailers could sell in stores. With those barriers now coming down, manufacturers are selling direct to consumers and leaving distributors out in the cold. In response to manufacturers selling to their customers, retailers have started making and selling their own products. The old food chain is eating itself.

It's about damn time.

This antiquated process was riddled with inefficiencies that resulted in a product selling for ten times what it cost to make, if not more. Every party that touched an item wanted a cut of the final pie, which meant the customer paid for a process that rewarded greed and unnecessary complexity. Once these parties started cutting each other out and began selling direct to consumers, we woke up and realized we'd been duped for decades.

In Canada, we have a popular grocery store that charges upwards of $25,000 per SKU for shelf space in its stores. Is it any wonder manufacturers are seeking a less expensive, more efficient way to sell their products? Big-box stores are losing to companies like Everlane, Warby Parker, and Bonobos, which have decried the inefficiencies of the old food chain and are passing savings on to their customers by putting products directly in their hands.

There are ripple effects coming out of this cannibalization of the food chain that I see every day because I work with retailers, manufacturers, and distributors. The big guys are so worried about other big guys eating them that they're making costly mistakes.

RETAILERS NEED TO FOCUS ON QUALITY

Large retailers who are mostly struggling to compete in an Amazon-dominated world are making a crucial mistake as they attempt to go vertical with their own products and thus increase their profit margins. Rather than creating unique, high-quality products, they're white-labeling shittier versions of products they already sell and flooding the marketplace with garbage. They're sacrificing quality for higher margins.

I recently bought some outdoor apparel from a mid-sized retailer here in Canada that cut its teeth selling great products from brands like Patagonia and North Face. When this retailer started making its own branded gear, I thought

I'd give it a try. To be fair, some of the clothing I bought was fine, but a lot of it fell apart at the seams after a year.

Patagonia and North Face strive to make the best possible products first, which means they're unlikely to make clothing that would fall apart this quickly. It goes against everything their brands represent. But, in the rush for higher margins, this retailer made the fatal mistake of pumping out shitty products. As an avid mountain biker and outdoor enthusiast, I'd rather pay more for a product that will hold up to the abuse of my sport for years to come.

Granted, a lot of people, including myself, still buy from this retailer for a variety of other reasons, but inferior quality will only take them so far down the road. Eventually your customers will turn on you and seek out better quality alternatives. If you're a retailer looking to build a business that lasts, you don't accomplish that by selling crap to your customers.

What retailers need to remember is that the barriers have come down for everyone, not just the big companies with deep pockets. Not even the giants in the industry are safe from the volume of new brands sprouting up and gaining traction in a fraction of the time it used to take to build a new brand. (Kickstarter, anyone?)

MANUFACTURERS ARE THINKING SHORT TERM

The fatal mistake I see manufacturers making is depending way too much on Amazon as a marketplace. Your direct-to-consumer strategy shouldn't be to sell on Amazon, because those are Amazon's customers you're selling to, not your own. A short-term revenue bump does not equal a long-term value creation strategy, especially when playground bullies like Amazon and Walmart will always look to squeeze margins out of manufacturers.

Another misstep manufacturers are making is going direct-to-consumer without being prepared for the challenges they'll face. They're used to loading trucks up with containers of product and selling to wholesalers and not selling a single item to one customer. Building a successful direct business isn't as easy as you might think. It takes time, and if brands are serious about going direct, they have to be honest about their shortcomings. There needs to be a focus on things like customer service (actual human beings talking to other human beings), returns and reverse logistics, strong content creation, traffic, and customer acquisition. To look at the process and say, "If the retailer can do it, it must be easy" is incredibly shortsighted.

You need a long-term strategy before you go direct, or else you're going to fall on your face. Yet, so many of these

$100-million manufacturers are selling direct but ignoring the strategy side, because $90 million of their sales are on the B2B side. That's all fine and dandy now, but in ten years, the manufacturers that don't create a long-term strategy for the B2C side will be up shit creek without a paddle, as retailers eat away their business.

The manufacturers I see that are going direct and being smart about it are doing very well. When the old food chain dissolves for good, they'll be the ones left standing.

WHOLESALERS ARE BEING INNOVATED OUT OF EXISTENCE

I've got friends who are wholesalers, and I fear for their future. Wholesalers exist because of an inefficiency in the broader commerce supply chain and utilize a business model built around low profit margins and high volume. They're brokers, and given the shifts in behavior from retailers and manufacturers, these brokers will eventually be innovated out of existence.

The shady way you see some wholesalers trying to survive is by selling products from their manufacturers on Amazon, thereby undercutting retailers. They'll set up another company they directly or indirectly own and sell products under that name.

Some wholesalers are adapting to this changing world by serving as product-makers for retailers and cutting manufacturers out of the equation. They're creating products for multiple retailers and promising better prices than manufacturers can offer. I know some wholesalers with a background in manufacturing, and this transition has been natural for them. Others have seen zero innovation in their business in the past three decades and are basically living on borrowed time.

Even the wholesalers that are adapting will face big changes down the road. The supply chain is improving every day. At some point, the single-store Main Street retailers will be able to order a small quantity of products from manufacturers willing and able to fulfill such orders. Think about it. If manufacturers are willing to ship one item to a customer, wouldn't it be a rational thought that they'd also be willing to ship ten of that same item to a mom-and-pop retailer, completely bypassing wholesale distribution? Right now, retailers still have to go through distribution channels to make this happen, but the day is coming where that will no longer be the case.

What becomes of wholesalers at that point will be fascinating to see.

LEGACY SYSTEMS CAN CAUSE RETAILERS TO STUMBLE

Regardless of whether you're a wholesaler, manufacturer, or retailer, your goal should be—consistently and profitably—to build a business that lasts. You can't hope to do that unless you know where your part of the food chain is headed. If you ignore the foundational shifts that are happening, you could make a decision now that will cut you off at the knees in three years. You have to think "long-term solution" and not "short-term fix."

Accurately reading the landscape and making the right moves is difficult when you're in retail. We're talking about a $22-trillion global commerce market that's been slow to move. A roadmap won't make your moves foolproof, but it will ensure that you're equipped with a long-term strategy that's been carefully considered. You also have to be adaptable in a commerce world that shifts every month, not every decade. The successful merchants of tomorrow will be nimble and able to pivot quickly from the parts of their business that aren't working or need improving.

Merchants get in trouble when they view their legacy technology, people, and processes as sunk costs rather than opportunities to improve. I mentioned earlier that Demac Media has worked with retailers who run the same accounting software my grandfather had twenty-five years ago. Legacy technology endures because retailers see it as fundamental to the way they do business, and they're terrified of replacing it.

What they fail to realize is that if you look out a decade, the people who know how to run these antiquated software systems are quite literally dying. By not transitioning slowly now, merchants are going to face an abrupt change when that day finally comes.

This doesn't even touch on the fact that most businesses have numerous competitors now that are all capable of doing the same things they are. While I'm not one to focus on what my competition is doing, it certainly doesn't hurt to make sure I'm not falling years behind them!

Other retailers tell me they have spent a bunch of money on their software, and they don't want to spend even more money replacing it. They see it as a sunk cost and, as many of us are guilty of doing, they'd rather continue down the path with their current technology or software, even if it's not the right path for them. I believe there exists a middle road where retailers can work around their existing technology. Not replace, not tear down, but move forward with technology that fills in the gaps you have.

Think about fortifying a dam with holes in it so that you can do more permanent work, work that will result in you replacing the old bits and pieces at some point in the future.

Legacy people become a problem when they stand by legacy processes that hold your company back. The hiring and training of new employees is one legacy process that needs to change immediately. The anonymous era of big-box stores gave birth to the idea that retailers should hire the cheapest possible, instead of the best possible, employees.

Here in Canada, we have a hugely popular department store that every Canadian has visited at some point in their lives. Whenever I went there as a kid, I remember always receiving excellent customer service. The people who worked in that store when I was growing up knew their shit. Recently, I visited this store and asked the employees a couple simple questions about tools, because I'm useless around the house.

Everyone I talked to stared at me like I was from another planet. Over the course of two decades, this store replaced its once-outstanding staff with minimum-wage workers whose sole purpose is to stock shelves and give the illusion that they are there to help. In reality, they are transient, temporary workers, since retail is no longer a career. They couldn't tell me where the tools were, let alone which tools

I should buy. Legacy people are the ones hiring employees of this caliber.

Retailers that focus more on cost than on quality are in for a rude awakening as the world returns to the place where quality matters. Amazon and the like will own the low-cost, high-volume game and the rest of us will have to focus on experience, inspiration, quality, and service. Retail desperately needs a new generation of leadership that understands what modern customers value and will start treating their people as assets and not just shelf-stockers.

Snuggle Bugz was able to open stores and compete against retailers like Toys "R" Us, because my friend hired a phenomenal staff, trained them well, and pays them what they're worth. His employees are fellow moms helping moms. They are people who know the product, use it, and can properly advise a customer on it. Now imagine trying to buy a car seat from a fifteen-year-old kid at Walmart.

There's no comparison to be made. Walmart exists to give you the cheapest possible price and not much else, and they're not the only big retailer that operates this way. The problem is that a new generation of consumers is emerging that would rather buy fewer goods of higher quality than spend less for items they'll quickly have to replace. The previous generation featured professional consumers who bought tons of shit, which enabled retailers to sell products like crazy without caring who bought them.

Those days are over. Retailers who explain away bad technology, people, or processes by saying, "That's how we've always done things," are headed for extinction. Those legacy systems might have gotten them this far, but they aren't what will keep them in business for the next fifty years. If you're a merchant looking to grow from $1 million to $20 million or $100 million, I'd advise you to look to your peers for advice instead of bygone big brands. The big brands may dominate conference stages because their names draw a crowd, but as someone who has worked with small, medium, and large retailers, I can tell you it's the larger ones that are struggling the most. Don't believe me? Hop on Google and have a look at which companies are closing the most stores.

IMPLICATIONS AT THE MICRO- AND MACRO-LEVELS

At the micro-level, the big trends affecting commerce create a huge opportunity for niche brands. While the big guys are distracted with replacing their legacy systems and worried about their competition eating them, niche brands can go in and take customers from the big guys. Tiny Devotions is a fantastic example of a niche brand that's winning by bringing a unique, high-quality product to a passionate, loyal audience.

Diana House's niche business will likely never be the next Amazon, but she's seizing the opportunity to add value to the world and provide a good living for herself and her team.

At the macro-level, we in commerce must realize we can't be everything to everyone, which is a tough pill for big brands to swallow. If you work for a billion-dollar brand, one of these Fortune 100 CPG companies, and you've historically had something for everyone, the future doesn't appear very bright. I say this for a few reasons.

Certain big brands still know their customers and are adept at speaking to them, but a lot have built themselves into 800-pound gorillas through consolidation and acquisitions. When that happens, these companies inevitably lose touch with their customers, and often their product goes to shit, because they're too focused on costs.

This also happens quite a bit with private equity-owned brands. You have to understand the private equity model and their motivations and interests to know that they are the very opposite of what your visionary entrepreneur is setting out to do.

If you want to stand out in the future of sameness, you have to stand for something to stand out and that starts with the customer. All the best software, the best people, and the best processes amount to nothing if you don't know who your best customers are and where to find them.

THE WINNING FORMULA INVOLVES PROPER SEQUENCING

Winning in the new world of commerce will look different depending on your goals. If you're like me and want to build the best business for your customers—not necessarily the biggest—then it's time to update your approach to building a commerce company.

We're not just manufacturers, wholesalers, and retailers. We need to understand that our product isn't just the things we sell, but rather the business itself. Once we understand that, we can iterate on it the same way we would any product, incrementally making it better along the way.

With Snuggle Bugz, for example, my friend's biggest strength is knowing what to focus on and when. He maintains laser focus on things that will really move the needle instead of worrying about small things that many people call "low-hanging fruit." When it comes to hiring a specific person, implementing a new technology, or going into a new channel, every move he makes is calculated. He wants to make sure he's creating the leverage he needs with each step and understands that implementing new pieces in the wrong order can lead to a less than optimal ROI.

As we'll see in the next chapter, he knows the winning formula depends on deploying the right tactics in the correct order to maximize their effectiveness. In other words, a roadmap.

THE SEQUENCE IS GREATER THAN THE COMPONENTS

I believe we are living in the golden age of Ecommerce, even though Ecommerce isn't really that old. As a result of the three trends we discussed in Chapter One, it has never been easier to start such a business.

There is a downside, however, to these massive shifts affecting the landscape—noise. The surge of new Ecommerce businesses has created a huge demand for platforms and products that make the lives of retailers easier and their businesses more profitable. Technology companies and solution providers are popping up every day to keep up with this white-hot demand. The variety of choice has grown exponentially, and like everything else where choice is abundant, it can be as much a gift as a burden. We often feel as if we're suffering from choice paralysis.

The Ecommerce ecosystem used to house a few hundred players that merchants could use to address the needs of their businesses. Now that ecosystem has swollen to more than 4,000 providers. Looking at the full list makes my head spin.

Now more than ever, building a successful Ecommerce business comes down to the proper sequence. Every merchant has access to the same advantages now. The ones that stick around deploy software, platforms, and other tools in a way that creates the leverage they need to move to the next step on their roadmap.

I've witnessed the importance of sequence firsthand during our work with Snuggle Bugz. If you have a kid, at some point you probably created a baby registry so friends and family could buy you presents for your baby shower. A good portion of the customers Snuggle Bugz receives come in through their baby registry, which has existed online and in-store since 2009. For the past four years, we've made no meaningful improvements to that registry experience.

Don't get me wrong, the registry works pretty well. After

four years, however, there are aspects of the registry that need upgrading. It's taken an incredible amount of discipline from Snuggle Bugz not to touch that part of the business for so long when it brings in a meaningful chunk of their new customers. So, why did they hold off for so long?

The sequence dictated by their roadmap prioritized a dozen other projects over the last four years that were needed to make the registry successful once it was upgraded. For example, a registry is only as good as the customer's ability to search and find products. There's no point in having a great registry experience if at the end of the day people can't find the stuff they want to add to that registry.

Snuggle Bugz sells upwards of 20,000 SKUs, which is a lot of product by most measures. One of the first steps in their sequence was cleaning up the merchandising side of their website and business. Four years ago, there wasn't even a full-time employee in the business working on data. Whatever product details the manufacturers gave us, we posted on the site.

Over time, as the business grew, that approach created non-financial business debt that Snuggle Bugz had to pay down before we could build the best-looking baby registry in the world. We've been making it easier for customers to find, evaluate, and select products to put on their registry the past four years. With every step forward, we laid more groundwork for the improved registry experience we'd eventually roll out.

When feedback on a major part of your business gets progressively worse, it can be tempting to chuck that roadmap out the window and fix the problem right away. For Snuggle Bugz, the situation with their registry was like seeing some part of their store on fire and saying, "We'll get to it later." The only thing that kept us on track was the fact that we had a very clear roadmap from the beginning, and as we iterated on it every quarter, we knew we had this registry thing in the backseat that needed attention. We just had other higher-priority items to tackle first.

Looking back now, I think, "Why the hell didn't we do this earlier? It's going to have such a positive impact on their business." Then I remember that if we had done this four years ago when Snuggle Bugz was a $2 million business, the impact would not have justified the investment. As an owner-operated business, Snuggle Bugz chose to devote their limited time and resources to other areas before tackling the registry. They care about obtaining and serving their customers, not gobbling up the competition and being the only player left in town. Their approach is customer experience-centric and it works.

I've learned so many lessons working with Snuggle Bugz, but none bigger than the importance of trusting your roadmap. There were so many times we could have gone off track and fixed something out of order, but it wouldn't have helped us achieve our objectives for that quarter or supported our bigger roadmap goals.

Funny enough, on the day I'm writing these words, we're doing a final run-through of the registry that's been four years in the making. Even funnier is the fact that I woke up this morning and something wasn't working. Last night, everything worked perfectly. I swear I almost threw my computer out the window. Turned out the problem was the ad blockers on our browsers. Go figure, right?

Welcome to Ecommerce—no matter your sequence, challenges await you!

COMMON PITFALLS MERCHANTS MUST AVOID

Working with merchants firsthand, I see some common pitfalls that cause even the most seasoned retailers to stumble. The three that pop up most frequently are:

- Falling victim to shiny object syndrome
- Not realizing that success falls on a spectrum
- Failing to do things in the right order

A roadmap doesn't make you immune to these landmines, so you have to be aware of them as you're following your sequence. These are the tempting detours that don't look all that threatening, but can quickly turn into huge time sucks and money drains.

The first pitfall is particularly lethal, because everyone loves the latest and greatest thing, especially when it comes from an amazing company like Facebook, Google, Snapchat, or (insert sexy tech company in the news all the time).

STEER CLEAR OF SHINY OBJECTS

Facebook is a juggernaut in our economy right now. They're leading the way on many products that will shape how we interact, communicate, and shop in the future. I love it, because Facebook is always trying something new. I'm sure deep down a consistent goal on their roadmap for each quarter is simply: BLOW PEOPLE'S MINDS.

Facebook's maniacal desire to constantly out-innovate itself has also caused me a great deal of strife, because they're on the fifth or sixth version of their Ecommerce offering. Every time Facebook rolls out a new commerce offering, whether it's a buy button or shoppable products in the newsfeed, I get bombarded with emails from people saying, "We have to get on Facebook. They just released this hot new thing."

This is a perfect example of what I like to call "shiny object syndrome." I've watched companies without a roadmap waste years hopping from one shiny object to another. When it's so cheap and easy to bolt something that you think can help you onto your business, the temptation is too great for some companies to resist, even if they have no reason for going down that road. Many of the companies that email me about Facebook's newest commerce offering have no presence on Facebook, but because they see it working for other companies that have put in the work to utilize Facebook Commerce, they assume the same approach will work for them. How many people do you know that like being told they need to do the hard work first?

In the commerce industry, I'm bombarded with success stories every day along the lines of: "Company X is doing some new thing with Pinterest and crushing it," or "How I made $1 million in eight months by only spending $500 on this one thing." The noise from the media, your customers, and other companies can be hard to ignore. Hell, I see my own clients falling victim to shiny object syndrome. They rush to capitalize on whatever craze everybody is talking about and lose sight of what they had planned. That's not to say roadmaps can't be flexible, but you have to remember that one of their core purposes is to help you foster discipline.

The problem with shiny objects has nothing to do with technology or marketplace. It's a people problem. If you don't have the people who really know how to work inside a channel like Facebook, you won't be successful. The sequence is so damn important in a world where there's a new sexy thing released every week. You can feel like you're falling behind, and for entrepreneurs that's one of the worst feelings.

Shiny object syndrome happens on the people side, too. If you go back a handful of years, there was this boom in growth-hacking and suddenly everybody was a growth-hacker. Before that, everybody was a social-media guru, and before that it was another craze that blew up. The roadmaps we'll build map out your channels, technology, and people. It's not just new software that can distract you.

Don't get me wrong—your sequence can include adding the latest and greatest thing for your business. I would just ask you as an entrepreneur and merchant to take an objective look at this latest and greatest thing to determine if it helps you achieve your goals for the quarter and the year. If not, put it in an icebox and think about adding it to your roadmap when it looks to provide the most leverage.

WHERE DOES YOUR SUCCESS FALL ON THE SPECTRUM?

When you're a merchant, the question you have to ask yourself regarding success is not, "Are we succeeding in this endeavor?" but rather, "How successful are we?"

You see, success and failure are not singular destinations where you're simply at one point or another. You have to look at success and failure existing on a very large spectrum. On one end, you can be super successful, and on the other end, you can be a giant failure. In between those extremes are varying degrees of success and failure.

Let's continue with our Facebook Commerce example to see how this works. Merchants come up to me and say, "We set up our Facebook store and our Facebook ads, and they are working great!"

Then I ask them, "What kind of ROAS are you seeing? How does that benchmark measure against your other channels and your competitors? Is it profitably 'working' or just vanity 'working?'"

The same goes when someone says something is broken or not working. Usually that means something isn't meeting an expectation, but rarely does it mean that something is truly not working, as in, not at all—zero results.

When I dig into the Facebook Commerce numbers for a $10-million company that does 500 orders a day and see that they're selling one thing a day on Facebook, I just shake my head. Technically, their Facebook paid acquisition channel is "working." But if you compare their results against the amount of money and time they spent setting up this channel and getting ready to acquire traffic and customers through Facebook, it's hard to call that one extra sale a "win."

Situations like these are made worse by the fact that these companies sometimes have a full-time person in charge of this channel, even when the company isn't ready to be there. By latching onto a shiny object—Facebook Commerce—these kinds of companies fail to follow the proper sequence for creating a Facebook channel and their success is limited as a result. Had they, for example, created a social presence and tested a whole bunch of different ads (messages) against a variety of audiences before they went all-in on this channel, Facebook Commerce would be profitably working for them.

They can claim it's successful, but we know where that success falls on the spectrum.

If you're wondering where on the spectrum you can find substantial success, I like the approach taken by the team at Basecamp (formerly 37signals). If you're in the software world at all, you know these guys. They're "internet famous" and have written a bunch of books. I love Basecamp because their approach to success is so pragmatic.

They aren't seeking growth for growth's sake. It has to be good business before it can be big business. I think it'd do retailers a lot of good to approach their business the same way. Being everywhere with mediocre results is a great way to build an unprofitable business. Conversely, don't try to be perfect at something before you move on to something else. Perfect is the enemy of done, and pragmatic thinking rules the day.

The reason I prefer this type of thinking and apply it within my own business is because the amount of work to finish that last 20 percent is disproportionate to the results you'll get from going all the way to 100 percent. Imagine that the next step on your roadmap is cleaning up the merchandising side of your business, like Snuggle Bugz had to do. Now I want you to imagine all the work that goes into that endeavor as a pie chart:

- The effort to go from 0 to 80 percent takes up 10 percent of that pie.
- The other 90 percent of the pie is what it takes to go from 80 to 100 percent.

It's not worth it to try to be the best at any one thing. You're better off moving quickly and pragmatically from one area to the next and building big support pillars for your business. The more pillars you have, the more prepared you are to achieve meaningful success.

So, before you tackle something like Facebook Commerce, ask yourself if that endeavor supports the current, broader objectives of your business. If it doesn't, move on to something else. Even if the answer is yes, ask yourself how much success you'll need for that effort to be worthwhile, given your time and monetary investments. If you have a satisfactory answer to both questions, the final step is placing that task on your roadmap.

IT'S ABOUT DOING THINGS IN THE RIGHT ORDER

Now that you know to avoid shiny objects and understand

that success and failure fall on a spectrum, the next pitfall to avoid is a bad approach. Let me ask you, if I started working with your company, and on day one I wanted to see your twelve-month marketing calendar, could you show me one? If the answer is yes, I'm going to buy you a beer when we do start working together. You're a retailer who has its shit together.

I wish I could say the same for every retailer I've worked with, but most of them can't even show me the marketing calendar for this month, let alone next month. Everything they do is reactive. I'm not just talking about $10 million companies here, but huge $500 million companies that have been around for thirty years. It's incredible that they're still in business, given that all they do is shoot from the hip and run around in a state of panic.

Yes, they're successful, but because of their approach, they're closer to being a failure than a huge success. If they stopped being reactive and instead chose to be proactive in their approach, their success would jump clear off the end of the spectrum.

A proactive approach begins at the highest level of your business and starts with a basic question: In a broad sense, what are your business goals for the next twelve months?

- Do you want to grow topline sales?
- Do you want to make the business more profitable?
- Do you want to improve repeat purchasers' conversion rates?
- Do you want to improve customer service?
- Do you want to implement a customer loyalty program across all channels?
- Do you want to build a referral program?

When you look back twelve months from now, what's the baseline goal you want to have accomplished in that span of time? Your roadmap is backed by this goal, and everything stems from how you're going to accomplish it. With Snuggle Bugz, we set a twelve-month goal to grow the business by 35 to 40 percent without sacrificing the bottom line too much. That's a difficult task, but again, we'll be happy if we get 80 percent of the way there.

Once we established our twelve-month objective, we had two main branches of action to pursue: Acquiring new customers and selling more to our existing customers.

I'm a big believer that every business needs to do both, but I think you need to focus on one or the other at any given time. The approach we've taken with Snuggle Bugz is that every quarter for the next twelve months, we'll rotate between retention and acquisition. As I'm writing this, we're focused for the next three months on retention and improving the year-one value for their existing customers. This approach doesn't mean we're turning off all the acquisition stuff we already have in place. That would be dumb.

What it means is that we're not focused on adding new channels to the business, the reason being that we feel we can dramatically move the needle if we improve what Snuggle Bugz already has in place. Like I mentioned at the beginning of this chapter, this kind of approach takes a great deal of restraint. There are a handful of big channels we're not currently in, and we know that if we entered those channels, it would add sales to the business and raise revenue. Yet, we're holding off for a good reason.

We know that this revenue would not be "good revenue." The cost to enter those channels now, given how our current funnels work and the way the business is set up, would hurt the bottom line and eventually starve Snuggle Bugz. It's a move that would hurt cash flow and impact the company's ability to make future investments. Entering those channels now would set off a harmful domino effect, so retention is our focus.

A roadmap that rotates between retention and acquisition in quarterly cycles throughout the year makes it much easier to operate with restraint. When someone comes to you and says, "I think we need to do this," you can look at your roadmap and validate that decision against current quarterly objectives. If it doesn't support those objectives, you can scrap that idea entirely or add it to the roadmap later if you think it's important. Having a roadmap takes emotion out of the decision-making process.

Roadmaps also help you deal with the HiPPO—the "highest-paid person's opinion."

My approach is to always try to get the HiPPO to sign off on all roadmap iterations. Keeping them informed will go a long way to ensuring they don't throw a hand grenade into your roadmap later. It also proves to them that you're planning every action the company is taking and measuring those actions against the key performance indicators (KPIs) that matter to your business. The effectiveness of the roadmap becomes undeniable at that point, and you'll have an easier time saying no to the HiPPO, because your roadmap backs up what you're saying. Instead of getting run over, you can stand your ground and follow the sequence you know will work.

If the HiPPO still steamrolls you at that point, you've got a shitty boss and there are bigger problems to address first. Some retail leaders are just not built for this digital-first commerce landscape and will be a problem until they leave or you leave. Find a better company that values the logical approach a roadmap provides.

WHY ROADMAPS ARE KING

Companies without a roadmap tend to jump from one idea to the next. They also love jumping to conclusions that aren't supported by data. Both types of jumping are bad, but if you ask me, faulty conclusions are more damaging to your company because they impact your approach moving forward. The trick is to fail fast and get data so you can iterate. Failure isn't bad; failure without learning is.

Statements like: "This is broken," and "That didn't work" are indicative of a company with a directionless approach. Talk to your customers. Actually, pick up the phone and talk to them, and I promise you'll be amazed by what you learn.

Whenever we launch a new feature within a company, we have a corresponding set of metrics that tells us the success rate of that feature. While far from perfect, this approach turns "This didn't work" into "This didn't work to our expectations. It achieved 15 percent lift in add-to-carts on the product page, but it didn't result in improving the actual cart-checkout process. We've got more people

adding to their carts, but we didn't actually improve sales."
This is an example of how I like to fail. It's specific, it has
data to support the feedback, and it gives us information
we can use to make better decisions later.

The ability to self-diagnose problems within your company is just one reason I say that roadmaps are king. I
also say that because roadmaps bridge the gap between
high-level business objectives and mercenary-level tactics
like sales funnels for paid media traffic. Roadmaps bring
together good strategy and good tactics and align them
up and down the organization with regards to your people,
processes, and technology. If you want efficiency within
your company, your ownership and executives must be
moving in the same direction as your line-level people
doing the day-to-day work.

Being in retail my entire life, I know how important it is
to get all your stakeholders on the same page. One way
I like to get everyone working toward a common goal is
to create a marketing calendar around big events that
happen throughout the year. If you're a merchant, you
know the dates I'm talking about. (Black Friday, anyone?)
You need to have a strategy in place for how you're going
to handle those days and list your goals for each event.
Your roadmap will support your marketing calendar, not
the other way around.

A roadmap exists to show you how to acquire customers for your business with the lowest cost and least resistance. It's that simple. While the idea of a roadmap comes from the software world, this is not something only technologists understand. Roadmaps are for anyone in retail who wants to grow their business in a healthy, disciplined manner.

Businesses without a roadmap can also grow, but in my experience, they're more like fish out of water—moving, but not very gracefully, and certainly not predictably. As a leader in your company, you don't want to reach the end of a month and say to yourself, "We didn't do anything this month." We both know that if you're uttering those words, you need to make some adjustments. A roadmap helps you avoid ending up in that situation, because you've got a sequence you're tracking against and goals you're trying to hit. If everything you do that month fails, you've at least learned something, which means you can do better next month.

I believe you'll succeed more than you fail, though, because roadmaps help you avoid bad strategies. Company ownership and shareholders can lay out an amazing vision for the company, but to actualize that vision, you need a strategic plan. From that strategic plan, you build a roadmap that turns into weekly and daily activities

Here's the order again: Vision—Strategic Plan—Yearly/
Quarterly Roadmap—Weekly/Daily Activities.

What's difficult in a $10 million company is for the day-
to-day people to know if they're moving the company in
the right direction. Again, it's about establishing priorities
that align management and ground-level folks. The execs
and ownership can validate their investment decisions
against the roadmap and know when they should hire
people, improve their processes, and add new technology.

The ground-level workers will know if they're moving
the company forward, because they can check their prog-
ress against the roadmap, which lays out expectations
and measurable outcomes for the next month, quarter,
year, and even three years down the road. As I said in the
introduction, the roadmap is the North Star that everyone
within your company can follow.

The roadmap is also crucial for dealing with external
partners. Most companies in today's marketplace work
with many different outside service providers and specialists, rather than having everyone they need on staff.
This brings up the question: How are you aligning those
partners with your business objectives?

Most companies don't prioritize this critical step in

the process. They try to manage the work that outside providers do for them, instead of showing those providers a roadmap that highlights their part of the process and asking for help. I don't know about you, but I'd rather empower an outside provider to do good work, instead of micromanaging their every move. The latter sounds exhausting.

Finally, roadmaps are king because they save you from talking about shit that doesn't need to be talked about, because it's on the roadmap. When you envision this document, don't picture it as the encyclopedia-thick business plans from the days of old. To be effective, roadmaps should be short and accessible. To download a copy of our roadmap templates, visit mattbertulli.com/commercecanvas.

ROADMAPS HELP YOU TARGET YOUR CUSTOMERS, NOT SOMEONE ELSE'S

Every retailer grapples with a couple of universal questions:

- How do we identify, target, and get in front of our ideal customer?
- Once we find them, how do we convert them into a buyer in whatever channel they are in? (Allowing them to buy anything, anywhere.)

That's the name of the game—and this book—right? Retailers can't serve everyone. You want to serve *your customer*, not the next guy's, which means you first must go out and find those customers. The problem now is that your customers are all over the place, spread across different channels and taking unique customer journeys.

As a retailer, the concept of "anything, anywhere" can feel overwhelming. Where the hell do you even get started? You guessed it—your roadmap, which helps you find your ideal customer by first identifying the channels they are most likely to frequent. Just because anything can be purchased anywhere now doesn't mean your brand and your products need to be everywhere. When you're starting out, you want to find the one channel where your ideal customers exist in large quantities. I call this your "big channel." In Chapter Three, we'll discuss big channels in depth and how you can eventually move beyond them to other, smaller channels.

Knowing who your ideal customers are and where to find them is still an inexact science. With Snuggle Bugz, we know who our customer is 80 percent of the time. The other 20 percent of the time, we might get somebody else's customer. The signs are obvious—lower order value or a customer who bought something because of a deal or sale and doesn't come back. Roadmaps help you avoid bleeding into other customer bases, since you know exactly what your ideal customers look like and where they hang out.

The key to entering new channels, as always, is the proper sequence. When beavers build a dam, they do things in a certain order. If they chucked all the wood into the water at the same time, that shit would be a mess. There'd probably be a giant mass of wood floating down the river being chased by some homeless beavers. (Forgive me, I'm Canadian and needed some kind of beaver reference in this book!)

Part of the reason that sequence is so important is that every channel requires a different approach. Facebook is different from Pinterest, which is different from a pop-up shop, which is different from a brick-and-mortar store, which is different from your products being sold at an airport kiosk. Each channel provides a different journey.

If those channels contain some of your ideal customers, you'll need the right set of tools to reach them and a unique people strategy for how your staff works that channel. You can't use a copy-and-paste approach for every channel. Not only is that lazy and ineffective, but it's wasting money you could be using to make your best-performing channel even more kick-ass. I understand that it's difficult to resist when you see your ideal customers hanging out in a channel you're not in, but you need to wait until you're ready to enter that channel with a meaningful and customized approach.

When that time comes and you begin going from channel to channel, go in an order that supports what you already have, instead of starting from scratch in channels that you shouldn't be entering yet. Build your dam in a way that utilizes the technology, people, and processes you've already invested in. Don't blindly chuck all your wood into the water and hope for the best.

If you're wondering what a proper sequence looks like, check out mattbertulli.com/commercecanvas to download examples and templates that we have developed out of working with our clients.

YOUR BIG CHANNEL AND HOW TO MOVE BEYOND IT

We know from Chapter Two that you should master one channel to the 80th percentile and then move on to the next channel. The problem for many merchants is that they can't move beyond the big channel that's driving 60 to 70 percent of their business. I've seen some companies that have 98 percent of their business coming from one channel.

This is just a bad strategy, whether you're an Ecommerce business or not. Relying so heavily on one source of customers makes your business vulnerable and significantly less valuable. You're especially vulnerable as an Ecommerce-only business if you can't move beyond your big channel, because most of the time you have little control over that channel.

Here's an example. Five years ago, you could quickly build a substantial business using nothing but Google's organic search. Companies using organic search as their main channel were flying high until a couple of years ago, when Google made significant changes to its search algorithms. (Penguin, anyone?) Within a year of these changes, thousands of these companies were wiped away because organic search represented 75 percent of their business, and when the algorithm cut that number in half, they were screwed.

This happened again with Facebook and their organic reach algorithms. Companies depending heavily on being able to cheaply reach a massive audience on Facebook organically were no doubt shocked to find out one day that Facebook throttled that organic reach in order to push brands to use their advertising platform and pay to reach that same audience.

It's easy to get comfortable within one channel when you're seeing success. But you can't afford to do so when someone else can decimate your whole business. You have to build other customer-acquisition pillars to support your business, because the big channel where you get the majority of your customers is a pretty significant liability and will cost you dearly at some point in the future.

If your main channel is Amazon, they're going to screw you over and smile while they're doing it. Just look at this quote from Amazon CEO Jeff Bezos: "Your margin is my opportunity."

Good Lord. If that isn't ruthless, I don't know what is.

If this isn't clear for you, what Bezos is saying is that in some way Amazon is going to rip the rug out from under your feet and take most, if not all, of your business away. The whole line of AmazonBasics products is designed for that sole purpose.

Take the mStand Laptop Stand from Rain Design, for instance. A story that made the rounds online in April 2016 shared how sales of Rain Design's popular laptop stand, which sold for $42.95 and was well reviewed, were suddenly undercut by a nearly identical AmazonBasics laptop stand that cost just $19.99. Rain Design wasn't happy about Amazon's move, but what could they do about it?

Your margin is Amazon's opportunity. That laptop stand

is one of thousands of AmazonBasics products that was created strictly to take market share from other companies. If your products sell like crazy on Amazon, I can almost guarantee a carbon copy of it will be sold under the AmazonBasics label at some point. Amazon has the power to cut you off at the knees, because they own the channel and the traffic coming through it.

If your company gets 90 percent of its business from Amazon, you should be worried. The CEO of your big channel has promised that he'll come at your profits like Jason from *Friday the 13th* and cut them down right in front of you. To rely on a channel that's promising to sell the same products I sell but for less, and sometimes even at a loss, just to get market share, would scare the hell out of me.

Make no mistake, we work with companies that sell tons of products on Amazon. As a channel, Amazon provides two amazing advantages:

1. It builds up volume and improves your buying power.
2. It significantly boosts awareness of your brand.

I'd never discourage a retailer from utilizing Amazon as a channel, once their roadmap indicates the timing is right. I would discourage retailers from thinking they can build a sustainable business on Amazon alone. Bezos has promised you that won't happen.

If you're in the vulnerable position of relying too much on a big channel like Amazon or other marketplaces right now, you must find a way to take back some of your customers and get them buying direct from you or through other channels. You won't get all of them, but if you can move a chunk to another channel and begin building that pillar, your company will be able to withstand the blow when your big channel makes significant changes that backfire.

HOW BULLETPROOF COFFEE MOVED
BEYOND ITS BIG CHANNEL

Dave Asprey is an incredible entrepreneur, and his company, Bulletproof Coffee, offers a great template for how to move beyond your big channel. I've been following this company for years, and recently I had the pleasure of meeting Dave at an event called Mastermind Talks. We sat next to each other and talked about how he built his company into a hugely successful operation. Dave's company is the definition of a content-first channel.

The first thing Dave did was create a proprietary product that allowed him to plant a stake in the ground. If you're going to build an Ecommerce company, one of my rules is that you need products that are uniquely yours that you can build a brand around.

When your coffee includes grass-fed butter and "Brain Octane oil," I'd say your brand is distinct. Bulletproof Coffee is sold through wholesale distribution channels direct on the company's website, and most recently, they opened the Bulletproof Coffee Shop in Santa Monica with a plan to add more locations. Dave and his team have made it possible to sell their coffee in multiple channels, but it obviously didn't start out that way.

In fact, Dave's journey started with his research and documenting what he discovered through a lot of "bio hacking." I'd go so far as to describe Bulletproof the brand as a publisher that monetizes the great content Dave creates by selling their products through multiple channels. In essence, Dave started out as a publisher who sold product. He owns his big channel and all the traffic coming to it. He is in a very strong position as a business that—if you didn't look closely—would seem like every other coffee or health product company.

But Dave didn't sit back and milk that cash cow to death. He leveraged the audience that he'd grown organically to move beyond this one big channel. The way he's handled that transition is seriously masterful from the outside looking in. This is still a business that doesn't look like much more than a series of content channels on the surface, but is quite brilliantly organized. I'm sure Dave and his team felt like they were running in a million different directions at times, but from the outside looking in, all I saw was a well-layered approach to growing a business that's worked beautifully.

Had Dave sat back and watched the money from one channel just roll in, his contentment would've eventually bitten him in the ass. A competitor could've come along and built a better, stronger business with a lower-priced product and sold more product than Bulletproof.

Dave didn't stop with one channel and neither should you. Entering new channels isn't just about making more money. A lot of times it's about strengthening what you already have in place. I've worked with companies that started out selling direct and went to eBay and Amazon to sell more product and increased their buying power. Even if the channel you're entering isn't the most profitable, if it ultimately helps you buy at better discounts from your suppliers, isn't that worth the investment?

PLACING OMNI-CHANNEL IN THE RIGHT CONTEXT

The focus on selling in multiple channels has attracted a

buzzword I loathe, but I'll share it because people unfortunately seem to like it: Omni-channel. Ugh.

I like the idea behind omni-channel, but in the words of Gary Vaynerchuk, "Marketers ruin everything." Omni-channel should be about creating the best customer experiences across all channels. What retailers have turned omni-channel into is a way for their physical store inventory to be available in some manner online. In other words, omni-channel was a term that gave physical retail space relevance in a digital-first world. When you say omni-channel now, the average retailer will think "reserve online and pick up in-store" or "order in-store and ship to customer." This whole approach is far too narrow in my opinion.

But because retailers were more concerned with saving their brick-and-mortar stores from impending disaster, this bastardized definition of omni-channel became the beacon of light and hope. I find this fear irrational and somewhat hilarious, since physical retail is still a giant portion of wallet-spend for customers. While there's an argument to be made that retail is over-built in the US, many retailers will continue to receive tremendous value from their physical locations.

Thankfully, I see the pendulum swinging the other way

with omni-channel now. Retailers are realizing that the scope of channels goes far beyond their physical and online stores. With that realization comes the acknowledgment that if your brand is going to be an omni-channel merchant, you must create the best possible customer experience in each of your channels. Inventory availability and accuracy is part of the customer experience, but it's not everything. I believe retailers are starting to understand this truth.

Another misconception that's slowly being cleared up is the belief that omni-channel means replicating the in-store experience to the online experience and vice versa. In-store and online shopping experiences are vastly different and the very thought of trying to make one look like the other is just ridiculous. Can you see how crystal clear a TV picture is online, or know for sure that swimsuit you want will look good on you based solely on how it fits the perfectly proportioned supermodel? Of course not. Can you shop from your couch in-store or avoid the sales pitch from that overeager employee who's looking to fatten up his commission check? Nope.

Virtual reality and other supporting technologies might soon bridge the gap between these two distinct experiences, but for now, omni-channel cannot be interpreted in this way. When you talk about omni-channel within your organization, use it within the context of creating the *best* possible customer experience in every channel, not the *same* experience.

As we know, every channel is different and requires a unique approach to give your customers the best possible encounter with your brand, no matter where they are. If you use omni-channel as intended, it'll drive the business forward with the proper focus.

UNDERSTANDING CUSTOMER JOURNEYS REQUIRES BOTH ART AND SCIENCE

Think back thirty years and envision what the customer's journey was like. It most likely started with the customer seeing an advertisement that made them aware of a certain brand. If they wanted to buy that brand's products, they'd visit a retail store. Depending on how that in-store experience went, they might purchase the product.

If you were in advertising or retail, these were the good old days of megaphone commerce. Now we know that customers aren't just reachable through expensive channels like television. They can buy anything, anywhere. It might be a stretch to say there's an infinite number of possible journeys a customer can take—I'm bad at this kind of math—but I'd say it's damn close. For comparison's sake, let's imagine a possible customer journey today.

This customer initially sees a product on the blog of someone who isn't a merchant. Because we're so inundated with advertising nowadays, this product doesn't cause an immediate "buy now" reaction just yet. But when they see someone post about that product on Facebook, or spot a tweet about it, or discover it on their favorite Pinterest board, now they're interested. That's when the research phase begins: Asking friends who have the product, consulting trusted review sites, reading customer reviews on Amazon, and so on.

If they decide to buy, a myriad of roads to purchasing spin out in front of them. Should they want to try and find the lowest possible price, they may head over to Amazon and buy it there with a wonderful same-day or slightly longer shipping option. Maybe they make a trip to their favorite retailer and pick it up that day. What if the company emails them a coupon because they opted-in as a first-time customer on their website? Depending on the customer and the situation that customer is in, each of the above options could be attractive. If the brand wants to get the sale, it may need to be in each of these above channels.

All the possible customer journeys remind me of those

choose-your-own-adventure books we used to read as kids. The straight-line path that existed thirty years ago, between the discovery of a new product and the purchase of that product, is long gone. Every journey is unique and equally important to your business. You must understand how customers arrived at your product and create meaningful touch points along the paths they're most likely to take. No, merchants can't be everywhere. But if you're not entering the channels where most of your customers are coming from and creating exceptional experiences for them there, you're leaving opportunity on the table.

So, how do you find out which journeys your customers are taking? I believe that begins with knowing your ideal customers inside and out. Some people call this building a customer avatar or customer persona. What's their age and gender, where did they go to school, what are their shopping behaviors, what beliefs are important to them, which social media networks are they most likely to use, and so forth. Of course, it helps quite a bit if you are your own ideal customer, like Diana House of Tiny Devotions.

A deep understanding of your customers helps you determine how they might arrive at your product. This is more of an art than a science, and while I always prefer the latter, I see value in envisioning your customer's possible journeys, because there is attribution data that can validate those hypotheses. As we'll see in a moment, attribution is still a tough nut to crack in the Ecommerce world, but I believe there are ways you can influence your customers and see how they respond. Based on that response, you can make assumptions that can be further tested and fleshed out.

Let me explain with an example. We're working with a company called Pela Case that sells biodegradable iPhone cases made from plant materials. This company sells in multiple channels, but recently we've been focusing on Facebook ad spend. What we noticed was that if we increased our ad spend on Facebook, our sales increased across all channels. When we dialed that ad spend back, overall sales decreased.

When we looked at Google Analytics, which does the best job it can possibly do in attributing dollars to source channels, a spike in Facebook ad spend increased sales from organic search. We were left scratching our heads at first, but after a while, we began to develop this idea of how ads on Facebook and other channels were connected across devices and part of the same customer's path to purchase (their journey).

We knew the journey started with customers seeing the ad on Facebook. Even more likely was that these customers were seeing the ads on their phones during their morning routines or while they procrastinated at work. They couldn't take action until their lunch break, or after work, at which point they'd hop on Google and search for Pela Case to read some reviews and eventually purchase.

We couldn't prove that was the exact journey Pela Case's customers were taking, but our experiment did prove customers weren't buying directly through Facebook the moment they saw the ad. Their journeys were fractured and indirect, leading to increased sales across all channels, instead of the one we were hoping to increase.

We could have easily been distracted by this lack of perfect channel attribution and gone ahead and started to try to solve the challenge by exploring things like session-stitching, but that wasn't part of our roadmap and, while imperfect, we had enough proof to validate our assumptions.

As a merchant, these kinds of journeys can be frustrating, because it's difficult to know the return you're getting on your ad spend. At the same time, gaining a deeper understanding of where your customers come from always benefits your company.

Within your big channel, you should have enough data

and customer feedback to know with 80 percent certainty what the customer journey looks like. This is far more science than art. Before you consider moving beyond that main channel—because that's when customer journeys become more about art—there are some KPIs you need to know. Only then can you transition into new channels with more than a blind leap of faith.

KNOW BEFORE YOU GO: THE KPIS THAT MATTER MOST

The first and most important metric a retailer needs to know is the lifetime value of a customer, or LTV. What's a customer worth to you? I look at this within four timeframes: thirty days, ninety days, an entire year, and a lifetime. The LTV is my baseline metric, because it determines how much I'm willing to spend to acquire customers, which also determines how much I'm willing to invest in technology, people, and other systems and processes to support my channels.

We'll cover this in more depth in the next chapter, but I don't like acquiring customers on a cost-per-order basis. But, if you're using that metric, I usually aim for a 3-to-1 return. So, for every $1 we spend on advertising, we expect $3 in revenue. That ratio is dependent on factors like your industry and gross profit margins, but I like a 3-to-1 return as a rule. We're using that ratio with Pela Case, for instance.

Two other KPIs that affect LTV are average order value and new subscriber rate. I like to see how the average order value changes as customers move through the timeframes I mentioned. Ideally, that order value would increase as first-time customers become repeat customers and trust your business with more of their hard-earned money.

New subscriber rate is important because subscribers are potential new customers. If you're spending too much acquiring them given their average order value, not converting them into customers, or simply not getting enough subscribers, you're in trouble.

In addition to customer data, I also like to know my gross profit margins on a category and product basis. That way, I can reasonably promote and market the right categories of products depending on the customer's journey.

If you don't track these KPIs, it's impossible to move from one channel to another predictably. Notice that I said "predictably." If you trust your gut when entering new channels, you'll probably fall somewhere between success and failure on the spectrum we talked about in Chapter Two. I'd rather stick to science and move into new channels with the data in hand that can help me make informed decisions. I'm also more likely to see real success within new channels, because I know which KPIs and metrics are leading indicators of success. KPIs, the frequency with which we track them, and their importance by category are what I use when I begin working with a new merchant. You can download that matrix and see the full list for yourself at mattbertulli.com/metrics.

THE CUSTOMER DESTINATION MATTERS
AS MUCH AS THE JOURNEY

A customer's journey has a huge impact on their lifetime value. For every company we work with, I group customers into three buckets: low-LTV, mid-LTV, and high-LTV.

A typical journey for low-LTV customers is this: They'll receive a discount via email or see it on social media, then they'll buy once with that discount, and they won't come back. The mid-LTV bucket is the most crowded. It's filled with customers who've made a few purchases but don't buy from you religiously. The goal is to move customers from that bucket into the high-LTV bucket, which is filled with the outlier customers who account for a significant chunk of your revenue, usually greater than 20 percent. You want that bucket to be overflowing because this is where your highest return on investment is. A dollar invested in activities servicing high-LTV customers is likely to produce much greater return as a percentage.

The ability to move your mid-customers up a tier comes down to understanding the typical journeys and flows that high-LTV customers follow. Again, understanding that journey is a mix of art and science, since attribution hasn't been completely figured out yet. But if you have your customer persona defined and intimately understood, you should be able to figure out with a reasonable degree of certainty what that high-LTV journey looks like. Let me give you an example.

If your high-LTV bucket is filled with luxury consumers who buy $10,000 purses, which channel will have those customers: First-class seating on an airplane or public-transportation buses?

Here's another example: You sell high-end fitness equipment and your mid-LTV bucket is filled with readers of two influential fitness blogs. Wouldn't it make sense that one of your channels be an affiliate partnership with those content creators? By hearing about your products from a source they trust, those mid-LTV customers can move up.

The goal isn't to transform mid-value customers into high-value customers by sheer force of will, but rather to find the uncommon commonalities in the journeys of those two customers and focus your efforts there. All consumers have habits that can be tracked, whether it be their favorite interest groups on social platforms, when they're most likely to make splashy purchases, or the channels they prefer for most of their research and discovery. The great thing about customers buying the same brand is that they likely have many habits in common.

Find those commonalities and enter the channels that will allow you to nudge mid-LTV customers to buy your products. At the same time, continue studying the high-LTV journey to discover new touch points they share with mid-LTV customers. When it comes to your customers, change is the only constant. Channels evolve over time and new ones emerge every day to snatch up swaths of your customer base.

But if you build your business around serving mid- and high-LTV customers, you'll be golden. Where you need to be careful is with your low-LTV customers. If you're paying too much to acquire customers who make one discounted purchase and disappear down the rabbit hole, you run the risk of growing fast while failing to make any money.

Companies like this can struggle to remain solvent and meet their long-term financial obligations. Tons of merchants fall into this camp. I think about Nasty Gal, the Ecommerce darling, founded in 2006 by Sophia Amoruso, that surpassed $300 million in revenue by the end of

2016. The company's five-year compound growth rate was an estimated 92.4 percent. The median growth rate for online apparel sites is 15.3 percent.

It's insane how fast they grew. Venture capitalists were in love with Nasty Gal and the company was even courted by Urban Outfitters. So, imagine the collective surprise when this white-hot retailer filed for bankruptcy in November 2016.

I can't say for sure what went wrong for Nasty Gal to end up in this situation, but it always struck me that they experienced phenomenal growth with only two physical stores. Their social media presence was out of this world with more than two million followers on Instagram and north of a million fans on Facebook. But I think the problem they ran into was finding and retaining mid- and high-LTV customers with the right product mix in the right channels where these customers were dominant. Nasty Gal undoubtedly knew their customers in the early days and followed a roadmap that took them from an eBay store that sold vintage clothing to a multi-channel Ecommerce juggernaut. They could probably tell you the exact journeys their customers took within each channel. I think their struggles came about because they attracted too many low-LTV customers who made them appear "successful" but kept them closer to the failure end of the spectrum.

As an Ecommerce guy, I hate to say it, but they might have been better off opening more stores and capturing a percentage of the massive brick-and-mortar wallet-spend.

Either way, there are some great lessons to be taken from the rise and fall of Nasty Gal. This was a company that blew up because it knew its customers better than its competition did, but failed to scale while holding onto this deep understanding of those same customers.

Another mistake Nasty Gal made was apparently hiring a lot of people from traditional retailers that didn't fit with the company, in terms of both culture and their capabilities.

ATTRIBUTION IS FLAWED BUT FUNDAMENTAL TO GROWTH

I've mentioned a couple of times now that attribution in the Ecommerce world is far from perfect. Here's how I know that to be true: Google's Digital Marketing Evangelist—what an awesome job title—Avinash Kaushik, who is a damn genius, has spoken and written recently about the challenges of attribution. When Avinash says something is a complicated subject, you know ordinary folks like me are going to struggle with it.

I've made peace with the fact that attribution is a long way from being a perfect science. Maybe Avinash and his team of Google geniuses will figure out how to track customers from one device to another across multiple channels, or know it's me making a purchase on my wife's phone and not her. I don't see it happening any time soon, so I don't worry too much about it.

It's frustrating not to know where every dollar comes from when we increase Facebook ad spend and sell more Pela Cases, but with most Ecommerce revenue, we have a solid understanding of where the money comes from. The tools are advanced now and they're getting better every day. Attribution is far from perfect, but Ecommerce wouldn't be a booming multibillion-dollar business if retailers had no idea where sales originated.

The big-picture goal with attribution is macro, not micro. You need to know which channels are working using a combination of art and science, because that feedback gives you a good indication of where to go next. You'll find that some channels are great for acquiring super-profitable customers in lower quantities, thereby giving you more revenue.

Other channels allow you to acquire larger quantities of less-profitable customers and boost your brand awareness. Building a business that is sustainable long-term means entering both kinds of channels in a sequence that's right for your business. A sequence requires discipline and the data to support your moving beyond your big channel, and this is where attribution comes in.

As we look forward to Chapter Four, where we'll begin building a roadmap for your business, remember that sequence is key to everything you do. Sustainable businesses add channels, technology, and people in the right order. They know when to move beyond their big channel and enter new channels in an order that creates leverage.

Sustainable businesses understand the sequence that delivers them paying customers and work to create meaningful touch points during those customer journeys. They validate every decision against their roadmap, use data to diagnose problems and validate real success, and discuss omni-channel within the proper context of fantastic customer experiences.

I understand that all of this is easier said than done, but I can't overstate the importance of building your Ecommerce business this way. I'm far from perfect at it myself, but with my roadmap in hand, I can avoid the trap of doing the *right things* at the *wrong time*.

If you're ready to get that same confidence while you

work to make your Ecommerce business better, let's start building your very own roadmap.

CREATING YOUR COMMERCE CANVAS PART 1: CHANNELS

We are splitting the creation of your roadmap into two parts—channels and technology—because it's such an involved process. The first part involves roadmapping your channels. There are several ways to begin this discussion, but I want to start with a hypothetical question and example similar to the ones we get from companies all the time at Demac Media.

"We're a high-end fashion brand that sells into wholesale channels and a little bit online. I want to grow my online sales without my wholesale accounts getting angry at me. What should I do?"

Our fashion designer needs to start with the Commerce Canvas.

Whenever we set about creating a roadmap for a client, we begin by examining what kind of business they are trying to build. Often, we meet B2B companies that make a product and sell it into a multitude of distribution channels. Those products usually wind up on the shelves of retailers and then in the hands of consumers. You know, typical old-world supply chain stuff. Then we see brand manufacturers that have always sold direct-to-consumer, while other companies are multi-brand retailers. Each type of business will have many options for how they create an effective roadmap. Our job is to create a channel sequence that makes sense for each company based on their individual objectives.

As we roadmap channels for our hypothetical fashion brand, we'll keep in mind a few important rules, the first of which is: Don't shoot the golden goose. The fashion brand's big channel is wholesale right now, and they can't jeopardize that relationship to grow their online sales. Commerce is just like any other industry, in that relationships are a vital part of building your business. When you move forward, you do so carefully.

Rule one has a second part: Don't shoot the golden goose,

but know the limits of where that goose can fly. Our fashion brand has figured out that in today's commerce world, you need to create and grow relationships directly with your customers. Our fashion brand has a tremendous opportunity if they can find a way to increase their online sales without pissing off their wholesaler. I would start by entering channels where their customers live and that their wholesaler isn't using. You can avoid shooting the golden goose, while also building bridges to reach your customers directly.

For example, one channel the fashion designer probably doesn't want to enter is Amazon. There's a good chance her retail partners are already selling in that channel, and if she were to come in and start selling her brand—maybe offering better promotions because she has more margin than they do—her retail partners' sales on Amazon would quickly take a hit. The revenue from Amazon might be tempting, but it's not worth ruining the relationship with her wholesale channel.

One factor to consider in this case is geography. If the fashion designer has a large concentration of wholesale and retail customers in one part of the country, she could look at selling to people in another part of the country. She could begin running pop-up shops in locations outside the current wholesaler and retailer radius.

On the digital side, I think it's fair for her to consider entering channels where her retail and wholesale partners are doing a shitty job representing her brand. After all, it's her brand name on the clothes. If she needs to enter a channel and create a brand experience that meets or exceeds what her customers expect, that channel should absolutely be on her roadmap.

Before we go any further with this example, I think it's important to define exactly what a channel is, since the commerce industry tends to default to a very narrow definition.

WHAT EXACTLY CONSTITUTES A CHANNEL?

I have a simple definition of a channel. Anywhere customers are—that's a channel. I can already see some of my friends in the commerce industry responding with a collective eye roll to this broad and loose definition, but we're living in a world where customers can buy anything, anywhere. Channels are all around us, but as merchants, we have to keep in mind that each channel's scope is limited in terms of what it can do for our businesses. We don't need to be in every single channel, we just need to be in the right ones in the right sequence.

One of the oldest and most obvious channels merchants

need to consider is the physical brick-and-mortar store. While I still think opening stores is an important part of a strong multi-channel strategy, I do recognize that stores are limited by geographic reach and can't be the sole focus for merchants anymore. Unless you're IKEA and people will drive hours to shop at your stores, you're only pulling in customers from a certain radius around your location. As we discussed in Chapter Three, Amazon can be a great channel because of its wide reach, but it also limits the control you have over the customer relationship, since technically, all customers buying your products on Amazon are Amazon customers. (Also, you run the risk of Amazon eating your lunch if your products sell too well!)

Planes, taxis, airports, bus stations, public parks—all are sales channels capable of serving a specific need for certain types of merchants. People's homes are channels. You can't kick down the door and start selling them vintage clothing, but the streaming devices and smart home assistants making their way into our homes are opening up this very important channel. We've all heard of the multi-level marketers—such as jewelry or Tupperware parties—that depend heavily on using the home as a channel.

Sales channels aren't the only type of channel, either. Twitter is a great example of a service channel where companies can address customer concerns. A great analogy for Twitter came from Tim Ferriss's podcast interview with David Heinemeier Hansson, the creator of Ruby on Rails, and founder and CTO of Basecamp. Hansson called Twitter everybody's pillow, because we grab it and scream into it or punch it when we're pissed about something. I just love that comparison. It's so perfectly apt.

I don't see Twitter as a channel where people go to discover products to buy, but one where customers come to vent, complain, or voice an opinion. Heck, sometimes that opinion is positive! All the big brands are on Twitter, because they have enough exposure that there are a lot of people tweeting at them and about them. Even if you're a smaller brand, you should be on Twitter to share information with customers and monitor for isolated bits of information. Your brand may never be trending, but if someone had a bad experience at one of your stores, that's information you need to know.

Certain channels are great for building brand awareness. Here we're talking about park benches, billboards, newspapers, magazines, and the like. On the digital side, you look at channels like Google's display network, which is notoriously terrible for commerce outside of retargeting. When was the last time you clicked on a random display ad and bought a product? Most people buy exclusively through the search network, so the display network exists to boost your brand awareness. That said, if you're a small merchant under $10 million, I'm not a huge fan of spending large amounts of money on brand awareness. I have been known to have a small budget allocated to some broad awareness ads on Facebook, but even those ads usually serve a purpose of building a retargeting audience. You're better off building such awareness while also focusing on actual commerce and making money.

We know from Chapter One that channels are multiplying like rabbits. As a merchant, you must be plugged in enough to stay on top of new channels, but disciplined enough to enter only those channels dictated by your roadmap. Even if all the cool kids are hanging out in this new channel, smoking cigarettes, and listening to rock and roll, you can't invest time and money in a channel that doesn't support your long-term objectives.

HOW TO BEGIN MAPPING CHANNELS

Now that we understand what constitutes a channel, we're ready to roadmap them for your business. If you haven't already, I encourage you to download a sample Commerce Canvas from our website: mattbertulli.com/commerce-canvas. You'll see how we lay things out visually, and the rest of this book will be an in-depth exploration of how you fill your canvas.

Remember, you want to create leverage in your business and entering channels in the right sequence is the best way to create leverage.

This is a three-part process that begins with mapping your strengths as a merchant. Every company is good at certain things. Some are great operators that have the back-end of their business on lock. Their warehouse is the cleanest facility you've ever seen and runs smoothly. When orders come in, they're shipped out in under an hour. Being a great operator is a huge strength to have as the retail world goes more digital.

Some merchants are amazing storytellers. They know how to create and distribute great content and build amazing marketing channels. I've worked with other companies whose biggest strength is that they provide world-class customer service.

You must be honest with yourself as you evaluate the strengths of your company, which means looking at your team to determine the areas in which you excel. Are you the best company ever at buying products and managing inventory, or are you mediocre in that area but kick ass when it comes to servicing your customers one-on-one?

Lay out all your team's strengths and weaknesses. The

reason you do this is because some channels require sophistication in areas where you're not yet sophisticated enough. A great example of why we map strengths and weaknesses comes from our work with Cosmo Music, a music supply retailer we've worked with for years that has a giant store (50,000+ square feet) in Toronto, Ontario, which I like to call, "Disneyland for musicians."

Cosmo Music is a family-owned business that's been around since 1968. These guys are amazing operators who already excel at managing products and providing top-notch customer service, but they're always looking to improve; they invest appropriately in the traditional side of their business.

When it was time to move beyond selling in-store and on their website, CosmoMusic.ca, they evaluated their strengths before deciding which channel to enter. Given that their product catalog contained more than 100,000 unique SKUs, we felt confident in their operational skills; they could without a doubt continue managing products with a new channel in the mix. Because they had invested heavily in technology to manage their back-end, we considered that a strength, as well.

Given those strengths, they saw Amazon as the best channel for Cosmo Music to enter next. The only box they didn't check for a move to Amazon was already being in other channels outside their stores and website. Even so, we still felt comfortable selling on Amazon, because the biggest challenge that channel presents—managing inventory—was perhaps Cosmo Music's biggest strength. Looking at this multi-brand retailer, you might second-guess a move to Amazon. I certainly did. But Cosmo Music was able to build much stronger buying power, gain more market share, and built their brand just by entering this new channel.

I have other merchants for whom trying to sell on Amazon or eBay would be like chewing on glass. These merchants are great marketers, but not great operators. They don't have the tools or the people to manage inventory across multiple channels, so creating this level of complexity in their business would be one of the last things I'd recommend them doing.

If you don't currently sell in third-party marketplaces, look at other customer-acquisition channels before entering the marketplace world. I see this as a very big step, and if you don't have the tools or the team in place, you could be headed for disaster. Get your feet wet by starting with a channel that doesn't require as much foundation-building legwork and won't be as unforgiving as channels like Amazon can be if you screw up.

You can work up to entering new channels that are outside your current capabilities, but it takes time. Start by hiring the people you need to enter challenging channels. You're only as good as your team. (We'll look in-depth at building a team in Chapter Six.)

Once those people are in place, invest in the technology your team needs to excel at their jobs and move you into challenging channels with as little friction as possible. A farmer can't grow food without tools, doctors can't save lives without surgical equipment, and merchants can't expand into new channels without technology that enables and supports their success.

When it comes to any retailer's technology, I first want to know what kind of enterprise resource planning (ERP) system software they're using—what they are working with in the back office, if you will. If you're like Cosmo Music, and you've invested in strong back-office software that allows you to manage multi-location inventory, all you have to do to enter a marketplace is add a new location in your ERP software and work with some kind of feed management tools. In terms of entering a marketplace channel, you've got the biggest corner piece of the puzzle already in place.

If you don't have an underlying platform that allows you

to allocate inventory to another location, your foray into Amazon, for example, will blow up in your face. Imagine that you tell Amazon you have one hundred of a certain product, but fail to mention that two other locations are also accessing that inventory. When Amazon sells one hundred products, and your other channels sell fifty of the same inventory, you're in deep shit. Not only did you just really piss some customers off by overcommitting to them, but I don't know of a faster way to get banned from Amazon's marketplace than mismanaging inventory. In this example, you not only made your customers mad, you potentially made Amazon's customers mad.

Big-time third-party marketplaces like Amazon don't play games when you screw around with their customers, since they're left dealing with the brand fallout. When I say it's important to map your strengths, I'm not joking. You must be ready with the tools and the team to seamlessly enter a channel where another company is the merchant of record, or handles all transactions.

What I've described above also works if you are entering a channel that isn't a marketplace. Let's look at another example: Facebook.

Let's put aside the fact that I still encounter a lot of merchants doing very little with Facebook's ad platform and focus on why and when a merchant should consider entering this channel.

I always find it easier to recognize when I shouldn't be doing something. As an avid mountain biker, I know my limits, and when I encounter an obstacle, I usually have a good idea whether I can clear it or not. The same goes for road mapping channels—you have to know your limits.

I've found Facebook to be a particularly great channel for acquiring relatively inexpensive traffic using a strong content creation and amplification strategy.

What this means for your roadmap is that if you don't currently have the "muscle" in your company to create quality content consistently, Facebook is likely not for you.

Facebook as a channel is downright amazing if you have the people capabilities to work with its ad platform. At the time of writing, this is my favorite ad platform to work with because it gives me the greatest range of capabilities. I also recognize that it has taken me a long time to become competent in, with lots of experimentation and more wasted ad budget than I'd care to admit.

SIMPLICITY OVER COMPLEXITY

Every channel has some degree of complexity that can easily be looked at on a spectrum. While it's not the right starting point for every merchant, setting up Google paid search is not too difficult to get started in. I see Amazon as being on the other end of the spectrum. Selling in their marketplace changes how you run your whole business, particularly if this is your first foray into marketplace selling. Comparatively, there's nothing simplistic about entering that channel.

Selling your products in another country can also be simple or complex, depending on your approach. You can easily sell online all over the world, shipping from one central distribution center, but if you start doing enough business in a region that you need to think about putting people and physical locations there, the discussion now includes fun topics like taxes, currency, and lots of legal and accounting overhead. Most often this is unnecessary complexity for companies going from $1 million to $20 million.

It's sexy to say you sell globally and distribute in different countries, but consider the operational challenges such a move creates for your business, and evaluate, based on your strengths, where that move falls on the spectrum from simple to complex.

Simple channels meet a couple of important criteria. First, you can reach customers smoothly and with minimal friction. Complex channels create unnecessary difficulty and distract your team from the stuff that matters, like selling to and servicing your customers in your existing channels.

Another hallmark of simple channels is that their impact on your existing systems is minimal. This is dependent on your entering a channel that's right for you, since what looks simple to Merchant X might look complex to Merchant Y. But if you did your homework, the channel you're entering shouldn't require a systems overhaul.

When you overlay your strengths with a desire to keep things simple, there will be some obvious channels that jump out at you. We're not even talking about cost of acquisition yet, which is the third piece of this discussion. Just by evaluating your strengths against the simplicity and complexity of a potential new channel, you're going to see which channels are logical next steps for your business.

Whether they're the right choice depends a lot on one final factor.

WHAT IS CUSTOMER ACQUISITION COSTING YOU?

We talked about a customer's lifetime value in Chapter

Three, and now we'll look at the flip side of that coin. **A customer's worth is equally dependent on what it cost to acquire them.** Finding a channel that is simple and plays to your strengths is nice, but if the cost to acquire customers is ridiculously high, it's not a good fit for your business. Smaller retailers must find the sweet spot between strengths, simplicity, and cost.

The chart below helps illustrate the balance you want to find between complexity and scale in any particular channel.

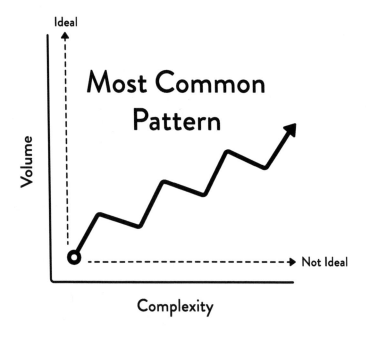

If you stray too far into channels that don't play to your strengths, you might be adding unnecessary complexity and giving up too much, and things will likely become unsustainable quickly. Complexity eats contribution margin and that ultimately eats away at your bottom line.

You need channels that are going to contribute to your bottom line while helping you grow the topline. You can chase buying power or market share after you've set up some channels that contribute to your cash flow. For smaller merchants, that's the top priority, because you can't afford to make mistakes. If you spend six months entering a channel that ultimately adds no bottom-line dollars to your company, you might not be in business much longer.

In working with hundreds of retailers, I'm amazed by how many of them confuse the cost of acquiring an order with the cost of acquiring a customer. Those two costs are vastly different, and retailers must understand what each means. If I spend $1 advertising a product and get a $5 sale in return, that's a 1-to-5 ratio on that order. But if that $1 investment brings a $5 sale with a monthly repeat purchase rate, that's a 1-to-60 ratio for that customer alone in a 12-month period.

Knowing your customer value at different intervals and

not just on the first purchase is essential to calculating LTV. When companies don't know those numbers, they default to cost-per-order, which is short-sighted. Those companies could be leaving wealthy, healthy customers at the table because they incorrectly perceive the cost of acquiring them on the initial order as being too expensive.

If you told most multi-brand retailers they had to spend $1 to make $5, they'd tell you to piss off. At the end of the day, most of those guys are barely putting 10 percent to their bottom line, so if you tell them to spend more than that on acquisition, they can't do it.

I have conversations every week with retailers who have no idea how to calculate the LTV of customers, let alone do this calculation on a per channel basis. But I don't entirely blame them for not knowing how because, up until recently, they didn't really think about lifetime value. Before sophisticated analytics packages came along and data mining started to become approachable for us normal humans, the only way to measure the lifetime value of a customer was through complex loyalty programs or credit cards that you, as the retailer, owned. Big merchants were usually the only ones who could afford such programs. With the democratization of technology, that barrier has fallen and every retailer can now track many data points per customer, including LTV, but some of these old-school retailers have yet to catch up. They are still concerned with cost per order.

The retailers who don't understand LTV are still using an old playbook. Beyond the science of putting a store in the right location so people can easily come by, their operation was more of an art. It never occurred to them to measure how often people came back and how much they spent. They intuitively knew because they'd see familiar faces all the time. If they had a loyalty program, they certainly weren't assigning costs to each acquired customer. Most mid- to large-scale brick-and-mortar-born retailers I've encountered in my career fall firmly into this category.

The new retail operating system probably seems too intricate for the old-school crowd. Even if they know that something like LTV is important, they choose not to build the muscle in people, technology, and process needed to calculate it. But if you're going to survive in this brave new retail world, you have to follow the new operating system and know these basic customer metrics.

The coolest part of this whole customer-value discussion is that it's only going to get easier to track these metrics within your business. The technology has come a long way in the past few decades, but it's far from perfect. If Silicon Valley can ever 100 percent figure out acquisition and attribution, I will take a week off work and celebrate the entire time.

As software improves to meet the needs of retailers, my hope is that we as retailers take some lessons from the software world and apply it to commerce. The way forward is for us to learn from other industries and not be stuck in our retail ways. The merchants who tell me they're doing $30 million in-store and another $30 million online—which is insane—because "they don't have a lot of competition" will soon have tons of competition. They can't forget that the barriers to entry have come down for everyone, not just them.

You'd have to be crazy not to want to acquire customers cost effectively and plug them into an email marketing engine that costs nothing comparatively. I don't know of a better way to turn your $1 investment in acquiring that customer into $30 in extra revenue during the life that customer stays with you.

If you're not acquiring your own customers directly at a low cost and tracking their value over different time intervals, you're behind the curve, which is a dangerous place to be in commerce these days. For help calculating your customer acquisition cost, visit mattbertulli.com/ccpa. We've got an awesome template that will walk you through the process.

THE CARDINAL RULE ALL MERCHANTS MUST KNOW

The cardinal rule for all merchants—and I use that term to include not just retailers, but manufacturers and wholesalers—is simple but powerful:

You need a repeatable, scalable method to reach your customers in each channel you choose to be in.

All merchants must know this cardinal rule, because it applies across the board. The walls between what we've traditionally called B2B and B2C are coming down. I say that because, at the end of the day, even if you're selling to another company and not to consumers, you're still selling to human beings who are making buying decisions.

It doesn't matter whether those decisions are made on behalf of a company or a household; you should still want to know how to reach them in effective and meaningful ways.

Manufacturers especially need to know how to reach retailers, because shelf space is limited and expensive. We talked earlier in this chapter about businesses that can't afford mistakes because their cash flow is fragile. Manufacturers can't afford mistakes because getting products onto store shelves requires an enormous cost.

For manufacturers just starting out, a national retail chain might not be the best first channel to enter. A smarter first step might be a smaller retailer or selling direct to customers, but both moves require knowledge of their customers' behavior.

A great example of this is Unbound Merino here in Toronto, Ontario. They didn't go out and make a product with the hopes of breaking it into the physical retail supply chain. Instead, they went to Indiegogo and pre-sold more than $300,000 worth of product directly to customers as their initial channel, then used this momentum to build a direct-to-consumer channel on their own site as their second roadmap step. They've focused on the right channels for the early-adopter customer they are trying to reach, and as a result, they've grown a hell of a lot faster than any brand I've seen go the traditional retail supply chain route.

Conversely, retailers need to understand what omni-channel really means, because they have a leg up in this anything, anywhere world. Unlike manufacturers or wholesalers, they have years of experience and know what it takes to reach and service customers. But if retailers cling to a playbook that's decades old and don't acknowledge the shifting landscape, that advantage is meaningless. Some retailers can still enjoy success with brick-and-mortar retail and zero (or very poor) online presence, but where do you think those retailers fall on the spectrum from success to failure?

Here's a better question: Where will they fall on that spectrum in five years? Ten years?

The new world of commerce is messier than the old one. The cannibalization of the food chain covered in Chapter One makes the lives and relationships between manufacturers, wholesalers, and retailers more complex than it's ever been. The one constant across the board is the need to reach customers wherever they might be found. New channels arise and old ones fall away every day, yet the need to find customers within them is ever-present.

The way to make sense of this rapidly changing world is with a roadmap. Only then can you distill the entire landscape into something your business can understand and use daily to reach the customers you know are out there.

TACTICS TO INCLUDE IN YOUR COMMERCE CANVAS

I never wanted this book to be about individual tactics. You could write entire books about SEO or Facebook ads, plus there are ninjas in those areas much more qualified than I am to teach you about them. That said, your roadmap will likely include some of these tactics, and I want to give you my thoughts on a few of the big ones you might choose to incorporate.

LOYALTY PROGRAMS AND REFERRALS

I don't like the traditional retail approach of rewarding customer loyalty with points or discounts. I'm much more into the idea of customer advocacy, or getting customers to refer their friends to you through product reviews, social reviews, social Q&A on your products, and so on. I see tremendous value in this tactic and put it on my roadmap early on so I can start building strong customer advocacy long-term for the business.

For example, with Pela Case, we have created a referral program where customers can get $3 donated to a charity of their choice for every customer they refer to Pela. We've created a program that speaks directly to the type of customer Pela targets.

If you're a brick-and-mortar retailer with dozens of stores, look at platforms like Social Annex to help you build loyalty programs that bridge online and offline channels.

There are countless articles and books written about customer loyalty by people far smarter and more experienced than I am. I'm simply recommending that loyalty be something you put a lot of time and energy into when considering where it should fall on your roadmap.

EMAIL MARKETING

Email is still king. Everybody seems to think that email is dead, but it's not. It's still killing it in the Ecommerce world. No other channel is more effective in terms of return on spend. I'm amazed by how many merchants don't use email to its fullest potential by either not using email at all or doing something like a monthly "newsletter." On the other end of the spectrum are merchants that spam their customers' inboxes with daily blasts trying to sell them shit they don't care about or need. Both approaches are misguided.

The point of email is to reach customers with the right message at the right time. The other day I got an email from J.Crew showing me women's boots. Seriously, what the hell? I've bought from them before and they're spamming me with deals on women's boots? As a customer, I'm annoyed. As a retailer, I'm flabbergasted. As a technologist, I know that my wife was likely looking at something on J.Crew's site using my laptop and J.Crew somehow segmented me into a list for women's boots. I'm just not loving the daily barrage of emails I get as a result.

My first rule is simple: I've got no choice but to use email to reach my customers, so I do it responsibly.

Even if the above rule sounds limiting, I still have a healthy arsenal of email tactics to put onto my roadmap and execute against. Here are some of my favorites:

- New Customer Welcome Series (usually a three-email sequence)
- New Subscriber Nurture Series
- Abandoned Cart Series (usually a two-email sequence)
- Post-Purchase Review Requests
- Post-Purchase Up-Sells
- Post-Purchase Referral/Loyalty Requests
- Customer Win-Back Sequence (haven't purchased in a while)
- Repeat Customer Thank You

Merchants break the first rule by regularly opting to email their entire list the exact same message. With the tools and technology available today, creating some basic segments shouldn't be a huge undertaking.

I'd recommend you use at least the following segments to get started on creating more personal email campaigns:

- High Value
- Medium Value
- Low Value
- Haven't Purchased in Six Months (Lapsed)

This book isn't meant to be an all-encompassing guide to email marketing, but hopefully the above will get you started on layering email marketing objectives into your roadmap.

If you are looking for additional email marketing resources, I recommend you check out the blogs and resources created by email platforms Klaviyo, MailChimp, and Bronto.

USER-GENERATED CONTENT FROM SOCIAL CHANNELS

I'm still surprised when I see brands fail to actively engage their fans, particularly when those brands have product that is visually supportive of user-generated content. Brands like World of Angus, Pela Case, Luxy Hair, and Pura Vida are using technology and a little process to activate their most engaged customers by gathering and sharing user-generated content.

This is low-hanging fruit for the right merchant. You can simply tap technology like YotPo or FourSixty and easily begin curating not just product reviews but also user-generated photography from Instagram. This is the best version of "social proof" for merchants. If you have great fans, tap into this powerful force!

PROMOTIONS, DISCOUNTS, MARKDOWNS

What you see too often with promotions is that merchants run the same promotion in every channel and usually they run the exact same promotions year in, year out. They use the same copy, artwork, and offer for one ad that gets blasted far and wide. I'm here to tell you: That shit doesn't work. Offline and online channels are far too different for a copy-and-paste approach to your promotions. I shouldn't even have to say it, but you really shouldn't be doing the same thing repeatedly year after year with promotions. The very last thing you want to do is train customers to always buy on sale.

Think about offline for a moment. It depends on the store, but I'd say that most of the time when someone is in a physical store, they are there to buy something. If they aren't there to buy something, your sales associates can work to convert a browser into a buyer on a 1:1 basis. Customer intent online varies, but for the most part, Ecommerce is about buying efficiently. Sure, some people are on your site looking to discover, dreaming about future purchases, and looking for inspiration. Ecommerce is becoming a better discovery medium every year, but it's still mostly a channel in which customers are looking to efficiently buy something specific, hence why Amazon is king of the hill. Nobody is more efficient at getting stuff to customers than Amazon.

I understand that some merchants use the same marketing and promotions approach for offline and online channels. They have limited resources. We all do. Depending on your internal systems, processes, and capabilities, tailoring campaigns per channel can be downright terrifying. I'm not judging merchants who take content from their latest email campaign and use it for their in-store flyer. I've been there. I don't like it, but I can understand why you might do this.

I simply want to point out a better approach to promotions that doesn't involve starting from scratch every time. I believe a best practice is to start with a baseline campaign idea that can be manipulated across each channel. You can use similar colors, images, or copy, but each placement should be tailored to utilize the strengths of each channel.

With social media, you might opt for something silly or outrageous that has the potential to go viral. Email needs to be concise and attention-getting. Flyers need punch to make them stand out from all the noise that assaults our eyeballs. Pop-up shops provide you with the option to cater to even more senses—for example, by using music. Each channel has elements that can be leveraged uniquely— use them!

To sum up: Baseline your promotions and build on the baseline for each additional channel you are pushing out to. Your customers expect consistency from your brand across different channels, but at the same time, they're savvy enough to know when you're simply megaphone-blasting them in all channels with the same thing.

THE "THREE BUCKET" APPROACH TO ROADMAP RESOURCE ALLOCATION

Whatever strategies, tools, or tactics you decide to put into your roadmap should fall into one of three buckets: Customer acquisition, customer retention, or feelings. In total, the acquisition and retention buckets should hold 90 percent of your budget. The feelings bucket is reserved for anything that your team suggests with the following preamble: "I feel like we should..." It's difficult to put tactics based on feelings on your roadmap, because they can be difficult to quantify and are usually shots in the dark.

However, I believe you need a feelings bucket, because there's still an art to retail that's hard to measure. We've also got to leave a place for entrepreneurs to be entrepreneurs and trust their instincts. I like to give my team room to act based on their gut reactions, but I keep that bucket at 10 percent to force them to focus on the other two buckets.

You'll find that organizing your tactics into these buckets and maintaining the proper ratio for each makes it much easier to integrate those tactics into your roadmap.

ROADMAPS BUILD MOMENTUM FOR YOUR BUSINESS

I decided to write this book because the retail world needs a new operating system, and I believe the roadmap—which I borrowed from the software world—is the operating system we need. Then again, I'm a software developer by trade so roadmaps are second nature to me. I've learned over the course of my retail career that not all merchants feel the same way about technology or anything technology-related. I realize there's still an art to retail that can't be quantified. I've seen it. I believe it. But I'd argue that, with the amount of actionable data we now have at our disposal, it's foolish to make feelings or emotions the primary driver for how you build your business. Retail is now 90 percent science and 10 percent art.

Old-school retailers push back against this sentiment

and argue that the art is still the most important thing. I hope this book shows them the value of a more scientific approach. I want to help them understand that you can achieve success if you take a few pages out of the tech start-up playbook and apply it to commerce. I understand that success stories exist of companies who struck gold using nothing but intuition. I see those companies as outliers who had the right product in the right market conditions at the right time.

I want to teach merchants a process that is repeatable and that values predictability, not one that encourages them to trust their gut and hope for the best. I want merchants to stop thinking that their product is the physical stuff they sell. Their product is the business itself and that product needs the attention and resources merchants give to the things they sell. All merchants need a roadmap, because the scope of their success goes beyond what's on their shelves.

Companies that validate their decisions against a roadmap generate momentum and gain traction more rapidly than companies without roadmaps. I've seen it too many times for the results to be a fluke. The success Cosmo Music has enjoyed illustrates the power of a roadmap, and although we touched on their story earlier, there's more to their journey I want to share. You can learn more about the sequence that generated tons of momentum for them at mattbertulli.com/cosmomusic. Best of all, we interviewed the team at Cosmo Music, so you can hear directly from them how their roadmap and the discipline to focus on creating leverage paved the way.

Now that we've mapped channels and created a sequence that works for your business, it's time for the second part of the roadmap process: Mapping technology.

CREATING YOUR COMMERCE CANVAS PART 2: TECHNOLOGY

In the last chapter, we looked at how to incorporate channels into your roadmap. Now it's time to layer in technology to support those channels. We focused on channels first because that sequence will largely dictate what tools and tech you need, not the other way around. Both are equally important, but technology should ultimately support what you're doing on the channel side.

I can't think of any other time in history when the idea of a technology roadmap has been this needed in commerce. Times have changed: The democratization of technology has taken innovative software out of the exclusive realm of the big guys and made it accessible to everyone. As I've said before, this is freaking amazing for entrepreneurs everywhere...but there is a downside to this leveling of the playing field. Not only does the average merchant now have thirty-six categories of technology running their company, but the ecosystem of products and services across those channels has ballooned from a few hundred vendors to a few thousand.

Too many merchants get bogged down in the selection of technology for their business or, worse, get distracted by shiny objects. I can't blame them, though. Having a specific technology need and wading into the marketplace now is like having a sweet tooth and visiting Willy Wonka's Chocolate Factory. In both instances, it's unlikely you'll make it out unscathed.

You can't have an Ecommerce business without technology, which means you have to get your hands dirty at some point. The smart merchant understands that technology does not power your growth, but rather enables it by removing friction, increasing efficiency, automating workflows, and making complex tasks simpler. With thousands of offerings spread across those thirty-six categories, the key is to focus on the software and systems that represent wise investments and align with your roadmap.

What we've found at Demac Media is that, while technology is no longer a competitive advantage for your business, it can be a disadvantage. Good software and systems won't lead to success on their own, but you do need them to achieve operational scale as your business grows.

A perfect example is something as simple as cart abandonment, since this is one issue merchants face that can be made worse by the wrong tech. There's data out there suggesting that nearly 75 percent of customers abandon their shopping carts before purchase. You're leaving a lot of money on the table if your email marketing platform doesn't easily give you the ability to recover those customers, especially if they decide to go buy elsewhere. Not only should it have cart abandonment recovery capabilities, but at the time of writing this book, I'd also expect it to have a very easy-to-configure set of flows.

This is why I push merchants to move beyond RFPs and feature checklists. The software industry has adapted to merchant procurement processes and we're now living in a world where it seems that every software company is claiming to do everything in an effort to "check the boxes."

If you're using the wrong tool for your business, or using the right tool in the wrong way, you're going to find that you'll get return on investment but it might not be the maximum return on the investment.

Like it or not, merchants have to build some muscle around technology in an increasingly digital-first commerce landscape, and that investment requires constant nurturing. This is a foreign concept to traditional brick-and-mortar-born merchants, who are used to investing in physical stores and other physical channels and not having to touch them for a decade.

Digital commerce doesn't allow for passivity. The technology you're using or that you need for your business changes monthly, if not daily. As an Ecommerce merchant, you have to think of yourself as a technology company to survive in today's market. How you build this new retail-focused muscle around technology is the subject of much debate in the commerce world.

Some merchants that have been in Ecommerce for more than ten years advocate for building your whole team in-house and handling everything yourselves. I disagree with this approach for one simple reason: It's too damn expensive. It's also far too slow for how fast the market is changing. If I'm running a $1 million business and trying to get to $20 million, I can't afford to hire thirty specialists to fill each of my needs. The in-house approach is not feasible for most mid-sized merchants.

If we look at technology as an investment merchants have to make, and we understand that most companies can't hire an in-house staff to handle their tech needs, then the question you have to answer is: How are you going to add the tools, technology, software, and people you need in an order that makes sense for your business? In other words, what do you do first and what do you do last? The concept of a roadmap is so damn important because you need something to frame these conversations, something that gives you structure.

Once you add all the core platforms and interchangeable supporting systems, how do you roadmap the technology inside your business so it supports your channel strategy, which in turn supports your overall marketing and business strategy? If you don't have the right answers to these questions, your daily operations can devolve into a bit of a reaction-driven mess. I've seen this countless times with merchants who overbought expensive platforms, or bolted on tools and systems to help run their business because everything is so much less expensive than it used to be. The problem is they had no idea how to use most of what they bought, and since it was all bolted together too quickly and in no particular sequence, they didn't maximize their return on these investments.

You don't need all thirty-six categories of software for your business, and you shouldn't buy the ones you do need all at once. When you invest in technology, the best way to support your channel roadmap is to start with a sequence that makes sense.

DON'T TRY TO WALK BEFORE YOU CAN CRAWL

As a recovering software engineer, maybe I'm a bit biased, but I think technology is easier to roadmap than channels if you have a basic understanding of the landscape. Channels steer the forward direction of your company. Each move requires research and a huge investment of time and money, since each move either creates leverage or takes away leverage. There's real pressure to choose your channels correctly.

Technology represents the components you add to enable your movement on the channel roadmap. These roadmaps work together to grow your business, but technology becomes easier to plan once you've laid out your channel strategy. Creating a sequence for your technology roadmap also includes a good deal of common sense.

Here's an obvious example: Would you implement live

chat on your website if you didn't have the people in place to answer requests? Unless you're looking to ignore your customers, probably not. Do you think it's a good idea to buy a content management system before you have a content creation process in place? I sure don't. These examples might sound silly, but it happens every day. Because the cost of "apps" has come down so dramatically, it has never been easier to just buy another $29-per-month app that winds up sitting idle, no different than a gym membership.

Although cheap and easy to implement, technology that doesn't currently fit your business is nothing more than a shiny object. Step away and move on to something that will have short-term impact.

The challenge is that not all technology choices are that obvious. Take, for instance, affiliate programs that offer you the chance to bring new customers to your business. You might be gung ho about starting such a program, but have you added the back-end software needed to handle reconciliation, returns, and paying affiliates? You can't afford to lay the track as the train is in motion. If you have affiliates as a channel on your roadmap, acquire the software you need to manage the program, test it with a few dedicated affiliates, and ramp it up slowly. Trust me, you'll be happy you did. The other option is to just outsource affiliates entirely.

Think about email for a moment. There are amazing providers, like Mailchimp, Constant Contact, Klaviyo, dotmailer, and Bronto, that are relatively inexpensive and easy to use. But it's not enough anymore to say you want to do "email marketing." That broad term now encompasses a handful of big-bucket subcategories you have to think about. Your roadmap can tell you when the timing is right to properly leverage email for your business. You might start off with a plug-and-play platform like MailChimp and then eventually move up to something like Bronto. My recommendation is to get what you need to support your roadmap, not what you think you might need in a few years, once you've scaled more. These types of systems are now so easy to plug in and out of your core platforms that you shouldn't be stuck in long evaluation cycles for supporting software like email platforms.

A technology roadmap is easier to create now than it's ever been, but the sheer selection that makes this process possible also adds a new layer of complexity. I try to reduce that complexity by being hyper diligent with my roadmap. I protect my roadmap like I protect time. Instead of accommodating everything, I only allow room for the technology my business truly needs and can use in the short and medium term. Rarely do I make investments that have time to return horizons of more than three years. The landscape is shifting too frequently, and

I need to make investments against my roadmap on a quarter-out basis.

For most mid-sized merchants, the list of software they need contains fewer than ten categories and is probably closer to five or six. There's no platform that can solve all your problems, but I firmly believe you should say "no" to everything except that small list of important shit your business cannot do without. What's left over is secondary and likely unimportant, especially for businesses going from $1 to $20 million in online sales. You can do a lot with a little in this business. The rest is shiny and distracting.

The two big technology buckets you need to fill are core platforms—those crucial to your business that are typically more expensive—and supporting components that you can bolt onto your business cheaply to fill a specific need. I'd say 80 percent of the technology you should add will go into the core platform bucket, as these platforms are maturing quickly in features and functionality and will cover the widest range of capabilities you'll need. These platforms are the lifeblood of your business, because the functions they perform are critical to your daily operations. They're also costly. For these reasons, it's imperative you choose the right platforms.

Let's look at what that means in a broad sense. Then we'll

dig into the specific order I recommend when adding software in the five most important categories.

CORE PLATFORMS HAVE A BRIGHT FUTURE

As with any investment, there are important considerations to make before investing in a core platform. I'm admittedly a software nerd and more meticulous in my research than other merchants, but I think everyone should look at the underlying technology stack used to build any piece of software and the talent pool behind it before making a purchase. For example, Shopify is built on Ruby on Rails, a popular programming language and framework with a giant global community of programmers who love to work on it. Any program built using Ruby on Rails immediately grabs my attention as I know that I will find tons of support when I need it.

Now flip that around. Some of the core platforms used by the biggest companies in the world run on Java, which is a pretty old programming language, comparatively speaking. I learned it in university in the late nineties. I've never met a developer coming out of school who said they liked programming Java and is looking forward to a career working with it. It's still a giant language with a decent global community, but the language is far from sexy these days. None of the kids getting into coding are rushing to work on platforms built using Java.

You should care about this stuff as a merchant. Where are all the cool kids building apps? Which platforms are making it fun for developers to work on their framework? Answers to these questions indicate which platforms have a bright future. You can't afford to buy software backed by a shrinking pool of people capable of writing in that language. That means that the cost of employing those people is only going to increase as the supply of them dwindles. Don't believe me? A little bit of research will show you that the older the language and the rarer the developer who knows that language, the more expensive it is to work with that developer. Do you also want to be hiring people who haven't kept up with the latest and greatest in innovation?

While this might sound obvious, many companies rely on legacy software whose programmers are old and dying off—literally and figuratively. The software's back end might as well come with a giant countdown clock. I'd be scared shitless if my investment had such a clear expiration date.

I want to invest in platforms like Shopify that attract talented developers who are constantly improving the platform's robust features. The app ecosystem on Shopify is healthy and backed by developers who are in it for the long haul, which is a huge comfort for merchants who are in it for the long haul as well. Both parties can work together as merchants follow the roadmaps they've designed. Community is what you want since community is where support is found.

If you add core platforms with poor underlying programming languages and a shallow developer talent pool, you're backing yourself into a bit of a corner. Core platforms represent huge investments and form the bedrock on which interchangeable components can be added later. Add all that up and you're facing a huge ordeal if obsolete core platforms must be replaced.

Your Ecommerce platform is one of these core platforms, but what about your CRM? Did you invest in a platform that will be around for a while? Many of the businesses we work with use Salesforce for their CRM. Like Shopify, Salesforce has a large developer and partner community and seems to have a bright future. While there is certainly a lot of legacy technology in the Salesforce stack, they've done a good enough job abstracting that away from developers working with and integrating to the platform that it matters less. However, Salesforce has pursued a very aggressive acquisition strategy in the past few years that has me a little worried. The scope of their product is now so wide that it can be a little confusing and sometimes incredibly costly to implement their products. They certainly weren't always this way.

Beyond the background research, you should evaluate technology and software to see if it meets your business's most important needs. If you need a new email marketing platform, for instance, boil your list of criteria down to no more than a handful of key requirements that have the largest impact in the short-term. Vendors love to brag about the full laundry list of features they offer, but you can't opt for software with far-reaching scope and mediocre effectiveness. You need a platform that checks your handful of important boxes and does so impressively. I like software companies that focus on doing a few things really well rather than a whole bunch of things adequately or less than adequately.

A great example of a software company that focuses on doing a few things well is Nosto. They narrowly focus on personalization for Ecommerce and don't mess with anything else. That's the type of technology company I like to work with because I know what I'm getting is their main focus, not an ancillary feature they added on to get into more RFP selection processes.

When you buy a piece of technology and it's mediocre at the things you need it to be excellent at, you might as well be bailing water out of a boat out with a hole-riddled bucket. You're going to spend too much time angrily working against the deficiencies of that product and not enough time doing things that are good for your business.

If you want to know the order to follow when selecting your core platforms, I've got you covered. My list isn't perfect, but it's a good place for you to start.

SELECTING THE SOFTWARE YOU NEED THE MOST

The order in which merchants should start to think about these core platforms depends on the complexity of their business and the channels they sell through.

The two most common sequences for systems as a business grows are:

BRICK-AND-MORTAR TO DIGITAL
ROADMAP FOR CORE PLATFORMS

1. Point of Sale (POS)
2. Accounting / Finance
3. Ecommerce Platform
4. ERP (once initial accounting platform is outgrown)

5. CRM (one view of customer)
6. Order Management (for multi-location, omni-channel retailers)

DIGITAL-FIRST TO BRICK-AND-MORTAR
ROADMAP FOR CORE PLATFORMS

1. Ecommerce Platform
2. Accounting / Finance
3. Point of Sale (POS)
4. ERP (once initial accounting platform is outgrown)
5. CRM (one view of customer)
6. Order Management (for multi-location, omni-channel retailers)

Note: These sequences are the likely order in which these types of companies usually implement things.

PRICING MODELS

Whether you're buying software as a service (SaaS) or on-premises software, you need to know if the platform has any triggers that could cause spikes in what you pay. Some enterprise Ecommerce platforms charge a percentage of sales or make you pay significantly more for spikes in traffic or sessions. Some have caps, while others have no restrictions at all. There are almost always hidden charges and although they aren't deal-breakers, you should know the full potential cost of everything you buy.

I'd advise that you ask for a full breakdown of all costs from any platform you are evaluating. If you aren't asked for it, be proactive and prepare some of your Google Analytics (or whatever tool you use) data to show them what your typical year looks like. Regular traffic, peak traffic, regular order volume, peak order volume, and average items per order are all things that should help you get to a real total cost of ownership for most platforms.

If you ever intend on opening more stores, ensure that POS platforms support multi-location inventory capabilities out of the box.

For any core platform, avoid buying based on name recognition alone. This goes for both the brand of the software company itself and the brands of the clients it likely flashes on all of its marketing and sales material. Some of the worst decisions we humans make are driven by ego rather than rational thinking. I've seen too many merchants buy Ecommerce platforms simply because an industry peer uses it, which is not surprising when you consider these same merchants were born in a brick-and-mortar world and simply followed each other from shopping mall to shopping mall. This was just the blind leading the blind.

A bigger company doesn't necessarily mean better software. The old adage "Nobody gets fired for hiring IBM" is just that—old.

Most retail businesses have 80 to 90 percent of the same requirements. That said, don't buy your core platforms based on what the rest of your industry peers use unless you have specific needs that only a point-solution could solve. You are assuming that your competitors and peers have made good decisions, which sounds kind of silly when you frame it this way. I assume that most businesses that have competition like to think they are better than their competition. So how does buying the same technology they have just because they have it support that statement? Do your own homework. Dig deeper.

HOW TO ROADMAP TECHNOLOGY

No two merchants have the same technology needs. I've laid out the sequence I default to when beginning any evaluation of purchasing core platforms, but to include a sequence for each category—plus the myriad of interchangeable components—would make this book 15,000 pages long. Not only would I never finish writing it, but it would be obsolete the minute it hit shelves. Ultimately, building a technology roadmap is the same as building a channel roadmap: You should worry less about evaluating individual components and focus more on laying everything out in the right sequence and ensuring it all works together.

To download examples of technology roadmaps we've made, visit mattbertulli.com/commercecanvas.

Examples aside, I'm going to provide you with some rules to help you on your journey. I've found the following information to be very helpful in establishing a baseline when I'm trying to figure out what technology I need and when.

STEP 1: HUMAN RESOURCES (PEOPLE)

We began with your team's strengths on the channels side, and we'll start in the same place with technology. Do you have someone on your staff who is tech-savvy or comes from a software background? How intricate are the platforms you're currently using? There's no right or wrong answer: We're simply looking for an honest evaluation.

If you went out and bought the most expensive and feature-rich enterprise resource planning system on the market, could your team members take full advantage of that core platform? Again, there's no shame in answering "no" to that question. If your team isn't ready yet, and you know you'll need that advanced ERP system in the future, your roadmap goals for the year should include getting your team to that level. Whether that means implementing new training for your existing employees or hiring a new team member is up to you.

In the meantime, you should start out with a less complicated, more affordable ERP system that checks the "easy to migrate to a new system" box. Such a system not only aligns with your channel roadmap, but also plays to your team's strengths.

Here's another example: Do you have someone on your team who's a data scientist or comes from a strong analytical background? If not, don't waste money on business-intelligence software that kicks out reports nobody on your team understands. Data is only good to have if it's actionable, and it can't be actionable if nobody can interpret it.

STEP 2: EXISTING SYSTEMS AND INFRASTRUCTURE

You also have to consider the impact of new technology on your existing systems. The trickiest part of having thirty-six software categories within a business is ensuring that those systems can integrate with each other when needed. Don't invest in new technology that doesn't integrate with your old systems, and always opt for new technology that is simple to set up and easy to integrate with. Investing time and money in setup and integration is a huge opportunity cost if you're a small business and not careful about which systems you're attempting to integrate.

For any core platform and for most supporting systems you intend to acquire, ensure they have mature, well-documented Web service API layers. This is a good indication that the system will be easy to integrate with when you need to automate the movement of data, which in today's world is usually often. If a company can't point you to developer documentation for how to integrate with their platform, run.

It's also important to consider where each application you implement overlaps with others. As I mentioned earlier, the ecosystem has been heavily fragmented, and as a result, there is a lot of overlap in features and functionality. Not only that, but often the overlap is coming from places you wouldn't normally expect.

For example, some email marketing platforms offer product recommendation capabilities on-site and not just email. Product recommendations are also part of the personalization category. Overlap forces you to decide if you need both or just one. If you need both, which product recommendation engine are you using?

STEP 3: IMPACT ON EXISTING PROCESSES

Aside from integration, target new technology that first improves your existing processes before you look to totally change existing processes. Deciding which processes need improving depends on the process, but if you've created a roadmap that has objectives and measurable outcomes, it will be significantly easier to identify bottlenecks in your business. For example, your roadmap might show that you need to improve your shipping turnaround from ten hours to two hours in order to get costs in line. As long as your shipping process isn't broken, you can add technology to your roadmap that gives you new tools to increase efficiency.

If you either don't have anything on your roadmap or don't have some basic metrics in place for this part of your business, there's no real way for you to quantitatively know that this process needs improvement.

In this example, which tools should you consider? Start by answering these questions:

- Does this tool play to the strengths of my team?
- Will it integrate quickly and easily with my existing shipping tools and processes?
- Does it meet my most important requirements?
- How dramatically will it improve our shipping process?

Only you can truly know your specific needs. The point of the roadmap is to give you a framework to help establish and then evaluate your needs. Go after tools that match up with your channels, business goals, and team's strengths. The whole point of technology is to support what you're doing, make your business run more smoothly, and ultimately to make your life easier. The last thing I'll say here is that if you have technology that you think is more of a headache than a help, step back, identify any metrics that could quantify this idea, and see if perception is reality. If it is, change.

ECS COFFEE MOVED QUICKLY BY STAYING FOCUSED

When I think about technology roadmaps, ECS Coffee jumps to mind. These guys have been in business more than twenty years and have undergone four or five massive, company-wide pivots. We started working with them seven years ago, when they were looking to go direct-to-consumer after building a big wholesale distribution business. I met the founder, Neil, who had asked us to come in and talk about going direct-to-consumer online.

At the time, Keurig and K-cups were just starting to gain significant traction and ECS Coffee was starting to sell a lot of these single cups. In addition to wholesale, they had started to open some retail stores. Our approach was to add the minimum amount of technology to get up and running quickly so we could test the market. ECS Coffee had a strong distribution business, so their big requirement was finding software that integrated with their warehouse and back-end systems. They didn't want to create an entirely new set of systems and processes for an unknown business.

ECS Coffee couldn't justify running out and hiring a bunch of people or overbuying technology. They run a lean team, so the technology we chose had to allow that small team to operate efficiently. They needed to do a lot with as little as possible.

Seven years ago, there wasn't an easy option like Shopify out there for building their Ecommerce platform. We weren't even using the term "roadmap" at that point! Our best choice was to use open-source software and piece a lot of stuff together manually. As we thought about what to add next, sequence was critical, because we didn't have the money and resources to pour thousands of dollars and man-hours into this effort.

We had to move quickly to get something out there we could test, so we started with a simple Ecommerce platform to get them going. We didn't even start with the full feature set of the platform, either. We chose only the things that met our one-year objectives.

Our next big step was adding introductory email marketing capabilities and testing various platforms that could help automate some of the manual work being done in this area. When we launched, traffic to the site from iPhones was around 10 percent, so we didn't prioritize a mobile app or a responsive website design until that number rose to 35 percent of traffic, even though there was a ton of noise in the industry about how critical it was that merchants have a mobile strategy. We knew enough that while it would have helped, it wasn't the highest-impact initiative for us at the time. It wasn't unimportant; it just wasn't most important. After that, we circled back to platform upgrades, updates, and implementing additional features.

At the time of this writing, ECS Coffee now runs multiple public-facing Ecommerce brands in partnership with some of their larger distributors. They're helping brands they sell go direct to consumer. We built some technology to help them manage sites for multiple front-facing brands, which was integrated into their back-end ERP. The software allowed them to split the orders out and make sure each item was associated with the right brand for now-obvious accounting and reconciliation reasons. ECS Coffee could have never added this kind of software right out of the gate. They had to work up to this point over several years.

What I admire about Neil, the company founder, is that although he understands the value of technology and where to use it, he's smart enough to realize there are things he doesn't know. When he looks at technology, he asks the hard questions: "Do we need another system inside our internal technology ecosystem, or can we do this manually until it hurts?"

Neil is rare in that he doesn't overbuy technology or get distracted by shiny objects. It bothers him when software salespeople try to convince him that their latest thing is going to drive his business forward. His answer is always along the lines of, "Let's put it on the roadmap and discuss it later. That's not a priority for us right now." The dude has laser focus.

I'd love to share more about Neil, his amazing team, and the business they've built with ECS Coffee. Like Cosmo Music, we've got an interview with the ECS Coffee folks up on our website. You can hear from them what it was like building their Ecommerce business back before we even knew what roadmaps were—visit mattbertulli.com/ecscoffee.

In the next chapter, we'll look at building a team in a way that supports your roadmap.

HOW TO BUILD A SMALL, HIGHLY EFFECTIVE TEAM FOR YOUR ECOMMERCE BUSINESS

———

With our channels and technology mapped out, it's time to bring those roadmaps to life by looking at the people side of commerce. The tried and true "right people, right seats" thinking that drives most successful businesses also applies to Ecommerce. Offline and online merchants alike need people with certain skillsets and experience to enable the business growth their roadmaps are supposed to lead to. Unfortunately, there's a growing people problem in commerce, particularly in consumer retail.

The explosive growth of online commerce is just one component of the booming digital economy. Every aspect of our lives is going digital, which means that merchants must now compete with the likes of Google, Facebook, and the start-up world for talented young professionals. The talent pool has widened, but most merchants I encounter seem to be focused on hiring "retail" people. I think this is a giant mistake and I'll explain why below. Finding the right person at the right time can be a challenge for merchants, but if you aren't even looking in the right place, it may as well be impossible.

The roles that individuals fill within your business, and the sequence in which you hire them are just as important as your technology and the channels you're building. All three work together to form the foundation of a strong business. A lot of retailers are still running on an old operating system and thinking about people in the wrong way. Given the foundational shifts in how people work now, the future of work is uncertain. Retailers can't worry about what positions in their company will look like in the future. They need the right people in the right seats now—not twenty years from now—to actualize the plans in their roadmaps.

Yet so many merchants fail miserably with the people side of their business for one simple reason: Their corporate structure *sucks*. This is another problem with the old operating system. A lot of brick-and-mortar-born merchants are still using the same structure they always have. If I could, I'd rip up the organizational charts of almost every merchant and reorganize all teams into two big buckets of focus to get them realigned. If you've been following along, you can probably guess what those buckets are: Customer acquisition and customer retention.

You might be thinking to yourself, "That's far too simplistic for my business." Depending on the size and scale of the merchant, you might be right. But I'd argue that for companies going from $1 million to $20 million, you can align an entire business—customer support, marketing, finance, procurement, retail—around these two major areas of focus. All functions in a business are involved in acquiring customers or retaining them. Allow me to validate a simpler approach by pointing out how the antiquated and ineffective structures of most retailers are absolutely killing their businesses.

THE OLD RETAIL COMPANY STRUCTURES NO LONGER WORK

I want you to imagine your favorite retailer. It can be any category, but think about all the different interactions you could have with that retailer—shopping in their stores, buying from their website, using their app, dealing with customer service, and so on. What do all these interactions have in common? They all happen with the same brand in the eyes of the customer. Good or bad, those interactions meld together and shape your feelings toward that retailer.

Across all channels, consumers see only one name. They don't see the divisions within a company, and frankly, they don't give a shit. Yet, retailers insist on taking a siloed approach to building their teams within their business. Brick-and-mortar retail is kept separate from the Ecommerce side of things, and too often these departments aren't totally aligned.

Let's take a quick pause. At this point, you might argue that merchants are focused on omni-channel to create a seamless experience for their customers and avoid this problem. While this might be true for some merchants, the reality is that omni-channel is focused mostly on technology and infrastructure, which tends to neglect the human side of this industry.

With a siloed approach, why would you expect district managers, store managers, and retail staff getting paid commissions to push people toward the company's Ecommerce site? That site is going to take away in-store sales and diminish the commission checks of those retail folks. People are going to protect their personal interests over those of the company, and I don't really blame them, do you? Companies that expect retail staff to go against their personal interests and push Ecommerce are delusional. There's an obvious conflict of interest there.

If you're a retailer with separate divisions and channels that aren't properly aligned to common objectives, your customer experience will be lackluster at best. Customers can't see the silos within your business, but they know something is off if their experience with your website is vastly different from their in-store experience. The old retail approach is bound to create internal turmoil that bubbles into public view. When each division within a company is forced to fight for budget share, the executives within those divisions aren't going to fight for what's best for the company. Their personal interests are too invested in getting recognized for as much revenue as possible for their department.

I know this because I've helped hire people for retailers. I usually have a pretty good handle on the roles and responsibilities, especially when it comes to digital-focused positions. But the question that continues to go unanswered is who this new hire is going to report to within the existing company structure. If their superior didn't have ownership over all the channels or lacked the incentive to make them all work together for the good of the company, the hire would usually have significant internal conflict to deal with.

I've seen Ecommerce departments within companies we've worked with report to all sorts of other divisions—operations, finance, marketing, and even the owner-operator. I've even seen Ecommerce divisions that didn't report to anybody! They were separate entities off to the side fighting for the resources they needed to survive. This might sound absurd, but it still happens.

You have to stop thinking of Ecommerce and these other channels as their own verticals that are siloed within the typical corporate structure, when in fact they cut across every facet of your business, including retail, manufacturing, fulfillment, and distribution. Companies achieve alignment only when divisions stop being...divisions. Imagine a basketball team whose players care more about scoring points than doing what it takes to help the team win. Do you think this team of lone wolves will win many games? I think any success they have will eventually be undone by their collective selfishness.

The old retail organizational structure is no different. When divisions care more about how well they're doing than how well the entire company is doing, it's the company that loses.

You can create alignment across your entire business by knocking down the silos and moving everything to cross-functional buckets, thus ensuring the business works as a cohesive unit. Throw out labels like logistics, customer service, marketing, or purchasing, and make everyone on your team define their roles by how much they influence either customer acquisition or customer retention. You might have some overlap in certain positions depending on your category, but these are the two functional accountability areas to organize your company around. This also means that compensation, more specifically incentive structures, are focused on creating great customer experiences across all channels.

We'll talk about how to specifically build your core digital-first team in a moment, but my preference for mid-sized merchants is to keep things as small as possible, usually three to eight people. If your team members have the necessary skills and they're in the right seats, you only need three to eight people to go from $1 million to $20 million as a merchant. Time and time again I've seen small teams vastly outperform large, overfunded ones.

When you're looking to add talent to your customer-acquisition bucket, focus on areas like content creation and distribution, channel management, catalog management, and sales-funnel design. The primary objective of the team members inside this bucket is to create a customer-acquisition process that can be optimized across all your channels.

Customer retention relies heavily on your onboarding process. Consider these questions:

- What happens when we get a new customer?
- What message do we send out to them?
- How does the product they ordered get shipped to them?
- What kind of love and care goes into that shipment?
- How do we convert subscribers into customers?

Building your in-house team with these two accountability areas in mind makes alignment a breeze. Creating a compensation structure that incentivizes holistic company growth also helps with alignment. If the whole company wins, everyone on your team should win. A monetary incentive can actually help to get people pulling in the same direction!

LOOK TO HIRE JOURNEYMEN AND GENERALISTS

If you're building a team of three to eight people and need to hire them in the right order, you've got to look for people with broad skillsets and prioritize the roles you need to fill. With that in mind, I suggest filling your in-house team with journeymen and generalists, folks capable of wearing multiple hats. Early on, you don't want team members with super-deep specialties like Google AdWords. You can use outside specialists to fill any gaps your team members don't cover.

When you hire these journeymen and generalists, look at them as traffic cops. Their job is to handle tons of activity in the areas of customer acquisition and retention. In addition to their in-house duties, traffic cops also coordinate with the third-party specialists handling areas like your affiliate marketing or order fulfillment.

Side note: It is often a distraction to own your warehouse and logistics operations if you're a mid-sized merchant. There are third-party logistics providers out there who can ship your stuff faster and more effectively than you can. Entrepreneurs who lack the depth of experience in operations should look to outsource this and focus instead on what they are good at, which is hopefully customer acquisition and retention.

Once you understand the types of people you should hire, the next step is filling roles in a sequence that builds leverage for your business. If I'm creating a digital team from scratch, the first position I want to hire is an Ecommerce manager. They need a basic understanding of digital marketing and its many forms. A background in merchandising is important, because how products are displayed to customers is critical now. It's nice if the candidate knows how customer-service teams work, although they won't do this work themselves. Most of all, I'd want an analytics person who can look at numbers and understand them. Businesses tend to operate beautifully when somebody has a good grasp of the data.

Once I've got an Ecommerce manager who's overseeing everything, I want a marketing traffic cop who can work with outside help on things like paid search, Facebook advertising, and affiliate marketing. I want somebody from the outset who owns customer acquisition. On the flip side, I also want somebody who can own customer retention. In my mind, that person is strong in customer service, email marketing, list management, and list segmentation.

Your first three hires should be digital-first people who understand data. Almost every business can benefit from this approach, because these folks can tend to your big-bucket needs of acquisition and retention. Your roadmap will tell you which seats to fill next, but I would start by filling these three seats. If you're interested in other positions you should hire and what those jobs might look like, visit mattbertulli.com/hiring and check out the job descriptions we have available for download. No matter what position you're looking to hire, I bet we've got a job description template you can use to get started. You know not to hire specialists in your small in-house team, but there's another group I tend to avoid when I'm growing an Ecommerce business: People with deep experience in traditional retail. While this sounds counterintuitive, I want people who bring fresh eyes, not existing biases, to a growing digital business.

Keep in mind, I'm saying to avoid specialists and retail folks if you're building a small team. When your business begins to scale and your team needs to grow, your roadmap might dictate that you need someone with a specialty or retail experience. I'm laying out some general parameters, not hard-and-fast rules. Ultimately, you know best the roles you need to fill and should decide what hats those team members need to wear.

You'll notice that I didn't cover things like purchasing, finance, retail store staff, and some other obvious roles that a lot of merchants have. My focus for this book is on merchants trying to scale from $1 million to $20 million through digital-first channels, so I'm assuming that companies in this range already have the obvious roles covered and are looking to build out what they need to scale.

START WITH GROUND-LEVEL, NOT HIGH-LEVEL, HIRES

Scaling a business from $1 million to $20 million requires hustle and tons of grunt work. Merchants aiming for this kind of growth need team members willing to roll up their sleeves and do the not-so-fun tasks that need to be done. In my mind, high-level executive types don't give you the return you need at this stage of your business growth. You need someone who can get on the ground and scrub the floors. Executives are more apt to hire someone else for that task.

This is another reason I tend to stay away from the guy or gal who's been in the industry fifteen years, because that person is in a different place career-wise. Unless they come to you and say they want to get back to the hustle, they're likely not a good fit for your business now. Again, we want the right seats filled now, not ten years from now.

I'm not shitting on high-level executives in general. I'm just sharing my own experiences in building teams during the early phases of business growth. Those roles become essential once growth creates operational scale challenges within your business. Small teams driving $5 million companies don't require a lot of management. But once you start to scale the human side of a business and your team grows ten times larger, you need strong leadership to manage larger, more complex teams.

I didn't have executives in my business until we'd grown to thirty people. Until that point, everyone was on small teams of three to five people that operated autonomously. Each team had a leader, but there were no execs running things. Now that we've hired almost one hundred people, I have an outstanding executive team that helps me manage everything.

Avoiding high-level hires and eschewing people with traditional retail experience puts a lot of pressure on merchants to hire multi-talented professionals. What skills are essential to building your team, and how do you find people with those skills? Let's find out.

One final note for merchants that are scaling, particularly those merchants with thriving Ecommerce businesses. There are a lot of "big résumé" people in the market who look as though they have a lot of experience at big Ecommerce companies. If you dig a little deeper, you'll find that most people with big résumés joined companies that had already achieved scale and weren't part of the smaller team who took that business from $1 million to $20 million and higher. In other words, there are a lot of managers in the Ecommerce world and not a lot of hustlers who did the hard work.

The guy or gal who was handed a multimillion-dollar

marketing budget at a big company is likely not the person to grow your Ecommerce company from $1 million to $20 million. This might seem obvious, but I still see small and mid-sized businesses hiring those "big résumé" folks and finding out the hard way that they have the wrong person.

HIRING: WHO, WHAT, WHEN, AND WHERE

When we begin working with merchants, the really smart ones will ask us, "What kind of team should I have? Who would you guys like to see internally if we were going to work with you?" These questions are indicative of individuals who have given some thought to team building and know just how critical people are in any business. Before we jump into specific traits you should look for, here are a few golden rules I give merchants who are hiring:

1. ALWAYS, ALWAYS, ALWAYS HIRE ON CULTURE FIT FIRST.

If I'm not willing to get a beer with the person I'm thinking about hiring, then I don't hire them, no matter how great they might be at their job. Life is short and shit will eventually hit the fan in every business. Your culture plays a big role in how those bumps in the road get handled. I'd rather go through the ups and downs with someone I can call a friend.

2. BE THE DUMBEST PERSON IN THE ROOM.

For me, this one is huge. Now that our company has grown, I hire specialists who are smarter than me when they're in their lane. I'm a generalist who understands enough about a wide range of stuff. That's my superpower. I'd rather focus on what I'm great at and give my team members the opportunity to unleash their superpowers in very specific ways every day. This creates massive leverage!

3. DON'T LET EGO CLOUD YOUR JUDGMENT.

Being in retail all my life, I've learned that ego can sometimes push people to want a team that simply agrees and follows orders. Yes-men and yes-women don't work for me. It's critical that I have a team that challenges me on my shit. Again, I'm aiming to be the dumbest person in the room. We'd be screwed if everyone always agreed with me!

The same goes for hiring outside contractors and vendors. Too often I encounter a retailer that asks for a referral to an expert in a specific area only to find out six months later that the retailer is trying to tell the expert how to do their job. What ego! Why hire an expert if you aren't going to trust them to be one?

4. START WITH TRAFFIC COPS.

Getting back to the specifics of team building, most of the time when merchants ask me how to build a team, I explain to them the concept of a traffic cop. Once they understand that, we look at skills that can serve their big-bucket needs. We mentioned these earlier, but let's revisit them in more detail and lay out some key performance indicators to keep in mind for each.

We'll start with acquisition and go over how to build a team that can cost-effectively acquire customers.

BUILD YOUR CONTENT TEAM

Content marketing is the bedrock of any Ecommerce business with its eye on long-term, sustainable growth. Content creation and distribution answers these questions: What message are you reaching customers with and how is it being delivered? I see this area being 90 percent about customer acquisition and 10 percent about customer retention.

For early stage companies, this is usually a role held by the entrepreneurs. For those trying to scale, it is also a good area to begin your team building, as quality content takes a significant amount of time to create and manage and can be done for a lower effective hourly rate than the entrepreneur is worth.

(If you want to learn more about effective hourly rates, or what your time is worth, I highly recommend a video from Dan Martell. Search YouTube for "How to Measure Your Daily Value Creation Score.")

If you're ready to add this role, here are some things to consider when looking for the right person:

- Content must be highly researched and data-driven. This means you need someone who, in addition to actually creating the content, can find topics to create content for.
- Balance among quality, speed, and consistency. High quality content takes time to produce, so you have to balance this against a frequency and consistency that your customer expects.
- Platforms for amplifying owned content are numerous, with Facebook being the big one. Whomever you hire also needs to have a decent handle on how content gets distributed and amplified.
- Some key performance indicators (KPIs) that this person might track are:
  - → Time on Site
  - → Leads Captured
  - → Visitor Funnel Progression (how far did they get?)
  - → Add-to-Carts
  - → Return on Ad Spend (ROAS)

CHANNEL AND INVENTORY MANAGER

There are so many channels available for merchants to sell into and service, and someone needs to own all of them. Target new team members capable of not only owning channels, but allocating and controlling inventory levels appropriately across the board.

This is another data-heavy role, so whoever sits in this seat is going to need very strong analytical capabilities.

Some KPIs that a channel management role might track are:

- Sell-Through by Channel
- Inventory Levels by Channel (allocation, shortages, returns, etc.)
- Channel Relationship Health Score (working with the people on the other side of each channel)
- Contribution Margin by Channel

CATALOG MANAGEMENT

For most merchants, especially multi-brand retailers, catalog management is a giant area of responsibility that straddles new customer acquisition and customer retention. This team member has ownership of your product-catalog data, from integrity to quality.

In addition to some data requirements, this person also needs to be very process-driven, as catalog management tends to involve things like onboarding new products, merchandising, and a bunch of procurement process-related items (supplier negotiation, lead times, quality control, seasonality, etc.).

The KPIs to consider here are:

- Average Time to List New Product
    - → How long from when a product is received to when it is listed for sale in all applicable channels?
- Completeness Score of Each Product (all necessary data for a specific item)
    - → Example: If the minimum number of complete data points per product is an average of eight, then you score your catalog based on the average of all products for these eight data points.

OWNERSHIP OF SALES FUNNEL EXPERIENCES

Your business will have numerous funnels, especially as you enter new channels. A good funnel should be continually optimized for the smoothest possible path to purchase. The goal of a funnel is to achieve a desired action. In Ecommerce, this usually means a sale, but it can often be an add-to-cart or a subscribe (lead gen).

Mastery over funnels is something that your modern-day merchant must have. I see this as the equivalent of strong in-store merchandising for brick-and-mortar retailers.

This is also a giant topic covered that entire books are written about, so I won't be going into all the nitty gritty details about what funnels are and how you should be thinking about them in the context of commerce.

What I want to do is give you a few pointers about the type of person you might want to put in this seat:

- Understands the relationship between where a visitor is acquired and where they land in the funnel. This is top-of-funnel optimization and usually the biggest impact lever to pull.
- Strong grasp of analytics.
- Decent copywriting skills.

Some of the things I like to measure with funnels are:

- Visitor Funnel Progression (which steps do they hit?)
  - → This is a fancy way of measuring conversion rate, but rather than measuring sitewide conversion rate, you want to measure how each step of your funnel converts a visitor to the next step.
- Average Order Value by Funnel

- Lifetime Value by Funnel
- Cost per Action (desired action)

Let's move to retention and see how we get existing customers to buy more from us.

PRIORITIZE THE ONBOARDING PROCESS

You want your retention team handling new customer onboarding. The opportunity isn't over just because a customer places an order. In fact, it's just the beginning. Make a great first impression on first-order fulfillment by doing something special for the customer.

Email is my go-to tool for onboarding new customers and ensuring they get the right flow of information at the right time. Social outreach is also a major asset.

LOOK FOR A LIST MANAGEMENT ROCKSTAR

Every great business—not just Ecommerce—should derive a significant portion of revenue from email marketing. All the low-hanging fruit should be accounted for, including:

- Post-Purchase Customer Engagement
- Loyalty Program Management
- Cart and Browse Abandonment

- Customer Onboarding
- List Growth, Segmentation, and Sanitation
- Acquisition Channel Management (where did you get the customer?)

When it comes to having a strong people strategy, if you narrow the scope of what you're looking for in a new position, the right person becomes a lot easier to find. You still need to seek out your ideal employees—this isn't a *Field of Dreams* "If you build it, they will come" situation—but when you shrink the pool of what you consider a qualified applicant, finding the right person becomes easier.

With some basic rules and guidelines in place, the next big question becomes where to find these types of people. I'll give you a few things to think about with respect to where you might find the right people for all of the roles you have to fill.

I start with the same people who are applying for jobs at software companies and digital agencies. I rarely start by looking for people with retail experience and never start with people who come from a heavy brick-and-mortar background and limited exposure to digital. The rub with looking for people in the same space as software and other digital companies is that the average young professional probably isn't looking for a commerce job.

They're simply not aware of how their digital-first skillset can benefit the average merchant. It's our job to reach out and educate them.

In other words, go where startups are recruiting people. Look for enthusiastic people who are actively engaged in the digital economy and have a strong read on the landscape. You very likely don't need to hire people with deep retail experience because that experience is largely irrelevant today. I would rather place my bet on the digitally native person who has learned to adapt to a fast-changing landscape than the person who spent a lot of time in the land of brick-and-mortar retail. I know this sounds a little black and white, although it really isn't. I'm a calculated risk and probability of success guy. I want to do the minimum amount of work for the best possible result, and when it comes to finding the right people, I use the above rules as my starting point.

When you speak the language of the digital economy—acquisition and retention—realize that this language doesn't mix with the old retail language. Kids coming out of school now would laugh at postings advertising a retail-centric job. Nobody that age knows what the hell a retail job looks like. They likely equate retail with seasonal or temporary work because that's what they were exposed to in their teens. They speak almost entirely in a digital economy-created language, so maybe it's time retailers start using the same language.

COMPLEXITY AND ITS IMPACT ON BUILDING YOUR TEAM

As I'm writing this, we're in the process of hiring an Ecommerce director for Snuggle Bugz. We've interviewed a ton of amazing candidates, but the question we keep asking is where this position fits inside the company: Marketing or operations? In my mind, an Ecommerce director should report to either a COO/VP of Operations or a CMO/VP of Marketing. We're still deciding between these, and I know other companies grapple with the same issue.

We all struggle, mainly because commerce is a complex industry going through a lot of changes. No two businesses look entirely the same once you step behind the curtain. I've worked with multimillion-dollar companies that sell 5,000 SKUs and ones that do the same dollar volume of sales by selling a few simple products. Complexity in commerce greatly impacts the critical roles within a company and the order in which those roles are filled.

For example, owners who are strong operators will often build a team that's strong on the marketing side to complement their skills. When strong marketers create

Ecommerce companies, they recruit generalists capable of propping up the operations side.

Complexity in commerce comes in many forms. Vast catalogs are even harder to untangle when you factor in the frequency of new products being added, longer buying cycles, and complex products with tons of features. Your supply chain can be an asset or a liability for a whole slew of reasons. Think about geography alone and its impact on your catalog. If you're selling outside your home country, what does it take to support those markets purely from the perspective of moving product around?

Logistics can be a nightmare. Are you shipping small or large items? Are they durable or fragile? Are return rates going to be a problem as you scale? How are you shipping orders? Running your own warehouse is both insane and rife with its own unique challenges.

The big buckets of acquisition and retention are finely tuned according to your margins and whether they're high or low. You also have to consider your customer LTV, and if your products have the potential for high repeat purchase rate or if they're the one-time-buy variety.

I apologize if all that made your head spin. My goal was to illustrate one final point about your people strategy:

Who you hire and when depends on many factors, each of which are unique to your business. I've worked with different companies that followed similar channel roadmaps and leveraged technology in roughly the same way, but I've never seen two companies fill the same seats in the same order.

The guidelines set forth in this chapter are rock solid. I've seen them work in dozens of companies spread across dozens of categories. That said, guidelines are merely there to guide you. I would never claim to know the foolproof strategy for building a team that could work within any business. I'd be living on a private island if that were the case!

Take everything we've covered in this chapter and synthesize it. Think about how it applies to your business and what unique challenges you face. When you're ready, consult your roadmap to see which seats you need to fill. It's the North Star that won't lead you astray.

Have you ever stopped to consider what happens in the future when every merchant learns to follow their own North Star? In the future of sameness, will roadmaps still give merchants an advantage, if everyone else has them? The answer is a resounding "yes." When everyone is driving down the same road, you need an inside track to leave your competitors in the dust. Chapter Seven shows us what the inside track looks like.

THE FUTURE OF SAMENESS

The idea for this book was born during discussions I had with my friends, partners, and customers about what I was labelling the "future of sameness." It went something like this: If technology is democratizing, and we can all sell in the same places for the same cost, with roughly the same design patterns, and the same types of people, the question becomes, "How the hell will the customer know the difference between all of us?"

The challenge, when everyone walks the same, talks the same, looks the same, and follows a similar path forward as you is this:

How can you differentiate yourself from the competition in this future?

We know the keys to starting a strong, future-proof Ecommerce business:

- Design a proprietary product, one that's not easily knocked off and has high margins.
- Become as vertically integrated as possible over time.
- Create a pricing model that is hard for competitors to replicate.
- Create the best possible customer experience in any channel you enter.
- Be your own publisher. Have a strong content creation and distribution strategy as early as possible.
- Build and nurture a lean team and equip them with the right tools to do a lot with a little.
- Keep your business as simple as possible for as long as possible.

Once you're established, continued success will come from the habits you instill—doing the little things right every day—and having the discipline to follow your roadmap. Think back to Snuggle Bugz and that agonizing wait to improve their baby registry. We all wanted to put that fire out sooner, but we waited until the time was right to invest in it. If you want to stand out, start by establishing habits and practicing discipline.

After all, just because a company has a roadmap doesn't mean they're following it. Have you ever switched off your GPS while driving because you thought you knew where you were, only to discover that you didn't and ended up embarrassingly lost? I'm guilty of such hubris, and I think merchants will suffer a similar fate if they ignore roadmaps and try to wing it.

There's still an art to retail, but the science is now more important to sustaining success. In a digital-first commerce landscape, merchants who prefer to trust their gut are probably just full of shit. The future of sameness demands that you have more predictability with a supporting, highly repeatable process that doesn't require a ton of oversight and overhead. A process like that doesn't just spring into existence on its own. It's created through the repeated execution of good habits.

Here's a great example: Every Monday morning, you and your team start the week by looking at the metrics that you're focused on improving for that quarter. If you instill that habit early on, those metrics will always be top-of-mind and empower your team to make smart decisions.

The discipline needed to create a repeatable, scalable business comes from building and exercising better habits—looking at the right data, at the right time, in the right sequence. Using that data to measure decisions against and to create a plan is a hallmark of proactive businesses. Reactionary businesses that make decisions off the cuff are driving down the road with their headlights off and likely aren't even trying to course-correct. They might not crash, but they're certainly tempting fate.

Roadmaps are only useful to companies that have built-in good habits, exercise discipline, use data to validate and make decisions, and have created a repeatable process. We've worked with a lot of merchants, and I can tell you that even if everyone has a roadmap in the future of sameness, half of them aren't built to utilize it fully. Even fewer will iterate on their roadmap and update their habits to match.

If you really want to future-proof your business, pick up a copy of Gino Wickman's *Traction* or *Scaling Up* by Verne Harnish. (Harnish's book *Mastering the Rockefeller Habits* is also great.) Both authors will teach you how to scale companies and the basic building block operating system you'll need. There's so much from those books that you can apply to retail, but I don't see many merchants starting or practicing these habits. The ones that do are brands I'll likely see twenty years from now.

PHYSICAL RETAIL WILL CONTINUE TO EVOLVE

A friend of mine recently said, "Every business I've ever owned cost me $600." If you're like me, a statement like that makes you stop and do a double-take. When I asked him to explain, he said, "It's simple: I buy a WordPress theme, pay for website hosting, and then start running content on the site." My friend was exactly right. It doesn't cost a lot to start a digital business today. Ask a retailer how much it cost to open his brick-and-mortar store, and, on the cheap end, it wouldn't be surprising to hear $250,000.

Stores are cost-prohibitive in that sense. But for multimillion-dollar businesses, opening a store is a move worth considering for the simple fact that, while expensive to open, stores make money. Why else would digital-first brands like Warby Parker and Bonobos be opening physical stores? As a channel, stores acquire customers, sell your product, and build your brand. Stores are profitable, which can't be said for a lot of digital channels, where the acquisition cost is too high or the average customer has a low LTV.

As we discussed in Chapter Four, a disadvantage of physical stores is that they have a limited geographic reach. They're only going to pull customers from a certain radius around the store, which is why store location is still so critical. Physical stores usually also come with a long-ass commitment on the lease. You can enter another channel and try it for six months. If it's not working, you dump it. A landlord isn't going to let you pull up stakes and move after a year, certainly not without a lot of fight and pain. Stores are as close to permanent as you get.

So, aside from profitability, why do we mess with stores? With Ecommerce growing at a rate of 20 to 30 percent a year, we know the smart move is building a digital-first roadmap to success. What future-proof merchants realize is that 10 percent of every dollar spent in retail is online, while 90 percent is offline. The offline growth rate is damn near flat, at 1 to 3 percent per year.

Online is eating offline, but it's not happening at such a pace that you need to hit the panic button if you're a mid-sized merchant with physical stores. The big guys are certainly in panic mode, because most of them are extremely over-built in their physical store footprint. We might be in the midst of an Ecommerce revolution, but commerce is still heavily rooted in bricks-and-mortar. Trade is inextricably linked to big global supply chains, and while we've seen some innovation there, we'll need a lot more disruption in order for commerce to be extricated from those networks.

In the future of sameness, smart retailers realize the best

customer-acquisition channel they have right now is their stores. Brick-and-mortar retailers stumble when they focus solely on the store and don't use it to acquire customers across all channels. As we look to a future where consumers can buy anything, anywhere, we merchants have to keep in mind the aspect of physical retail that offers the most leverage—human connection.

Let's get back to the basics and use our physical stores to really "wow" customers. Focus on being a great physical retailer and use that channel to grow your online business. Instead of worrying that your stores are dying because Ecommerce is eating the world, take a step back and realize that what you're seeing is evolution, not doomsday.

In the future of sameness, there will always be a place for stores. The evolution we'll see is that stores will become more experiential in nature. Entertaining customers will become a big focus as digital continues to creep more into our lives. No technology can replace the in-store experience at this point. Even next-gen tech like VR and augmented reality, which will be very cool at some point, will take time to impact the brick-and-mortar customer experience.

Other technology that improves the in-store experience for customers will continue to evolve as well. Some merchants we talk to still haven't mastered mobile commerce after a decade of effort. The ones who have an actual mobile strategy in place have a huge advantage over the competitors who are merely checking off the mobile box. The internet of things will bring us advances like smart dressing rooms, but for physical retailers that aren't proficient with technology, those advances are nothing more than shiny objects.

Smart retailers that will excel in the future of sameness take a step back from the noise and focus on building up areas of their businesses as dictated by their roadmaps. Offline and online, future-proof merchants are disciplined enough not to get distracted.

Don't misunderstand me: I'm not advocating that you shoot technology the middle finger and keep doing what you're doing. Smart merchants don't sit idly by and get blindsided by big changes. They cut through the hype to see what's important now, what's going to be important down the road, and prioritize. I said earlier that you can't do everything, and for some entrepreneurs, that's a real struggle. My advice is to figure out the big changes that apply to your business and address them in a sequence that fits your roadmap.

Don't get swept away in the "Uber-fication" of everything.

The pace of innovation and change is picking up speed, but physical retail is still king. Be pragmatic, pick your spots strategically, and you'll be smelling like roses in the future of sameness.

THE WAY FORWARD FOR SNUGGLE BUGZ

To close this book out, I want to revisit Snuggle Bugz and share how they're adapting to the future of sameness. As a multi-brand retailer, they're in the same worrisome place as big names like Macy's and Saks Fifth Avenue. Amazon is the playground bully taking their lunch money: Of every dollar spent online, Amazon owns roughly half. Not only that, but the brands Snuggle Bugz sells are going direct-to-consumer, which puts even more pressure on their business.

In the future of sameness, Snuggle Bugz is choosing to stand out with their digital-first roadmap, which to them means a customer-first roadmap. Everything they do revolves around creating the best possible experience for the moms they serve. New and expecting mothers have enough to worry about, so Snuggle Bugz is dedicated to making the lives of moms easier and helping them enter motherhood with as little friction as possible.

Ben Burmaster, president and founder, uses his company's

roadmap to support its crystal-clear vision and mission. Ben doesn't ask, "How do I make more money?" He wants to know how he can serve his customers in a better, more effective way.

Having a clear vision and mission is foundational to building any business, not just one in the commerce industry. What we've found is that companies experience pain when they serve their own purposes and not their customers. They're focusing on themselves too much when hiring new people, adding technology, and entering new channels. Once their focus shifts back to where it needs to be—the customer—the pain goes away.

Retailers that thrive in the future of sameness base their roadmaps on the knowledge of who their ideal customers are and how they can best serve them. Snuggle Bugz doesn't try to serve the moms who shop at Babies "R" Us. Ben and his team know their moms place more emphasis on connection and service than commodity. Every step on their roadmap is dictated by how they can fill those needs in meaningful ways.

For example, Snuggle Bugz has been making a concerted effort recently to speak to their customers better on Facebook. They've built up a passionate following of people who love the brand, but, until now, Facebook hasn't been a focal point for them. We're shifting their approach in the first few quarters of 2017 away from running ads and targeting everyone we think is in their audience. Our new approach is creating content that is truly helpful to new mothers and pregnant women. We're adding new tools to build that channel, but all the technology in the world can't help you if you sound like a selfish, shitty company.

By leveraging new tools to better serve their customers on Facebook, Snuggle Bugz is approaching the democratization of technology in the right way. The wrong approach is to view technology as a money-saving mechanism that increases your profit and allows you to cut staff. Companies should take the approach Snuggle Bugz does: Use the resources technology saves you to hire people who can help you better serve your customers.

How do you differentiate your business in the future of sameness? Do a better job than your competitors at serving your customers. If you create and iterate on your own roadmap to support a strong customer experience, your chances of success increase dramatically.

I've seen Ben and his team say no to technology that would've made their lives easier and saved them tons of money. Why? It would have hurt the customer experience. Some merchants who read this will fundamentally disagree with their approach, but Ben knew that automating something like customer service would've removed the human touch to his brand, and he wasn't willing to give that up. The human connection customers get with Snuggle Bugz makes the company stand out and is vital to its long-term success.

How can you serve your customers in a way that makes you stand out? If you're worried about the future of sameness, answering that question will show you the way forward.

FINAL TAKEAWAYS

By creating your roadmap, you've laid a strong foundation for your business. You now have a strategy for channels and technology, as well as team building. With a strong strategy comes alignment across all facets of your business, a clear focus, and better tactical execution. When you make decisions, you can measure the results against your roadmap. Unlike a business plan, roadmaps are ever-evolving to serve your business, where it is, and where it's going. Your roadmap tells you what to do and when to do it.

The "when" of commerce, as we know, is critical. The smart merchant knows that the sequence you follow is now more important than what you do. Every merchant has access to the same advantages as you. But with your roadmap, you now know the channels your business needs to be in and when to enter them. While other merchants blindly make decisions without justification, your actions are strategic and precise.

By mapping your technology to support your channel strategy, you know the technology you need to acquire and have the discipline to avoid shiny objects. The correct channel and technology sequence empowers you with the knowledge of the people you need on your team, what seats they should fill, and when you need to fill them.

I see plenty of merchants who busy themselves with the wrong metrics and making decisions based on the wrong data. With a roadmap, you know what to measure and when to leverage that data into further action. Not only that, but you have the people on your team who can interpret the data you gather, because you built your team in the right order. Again, good roadmaps promote alignment within your business.

If you take away just one thing from this book, let it be the idea that your roadmap is the North Star for your business. The path from where you are now to where you want to be is created when you map your channels, figure out the technologies to support them, and hire the people you need to implement your process. I personally guarantee that following those steps will fundamentally shift the way you run your business.

LET ME KNOW HOW I CAN HELP YOU

If you have any questions, I'd love to hear from you. When your roadmap transforms your business and you start seeing consistent growth, find me on Twitter @mbertulli or at mattbertulli.com. Nothing makes me happier than the success stories I hear from merchants crushing it, so please hit me up. I love this stuff!

When people ask me what I do for a living, I tell them I'm a student of, and evangelist for, retail. I try to learn something new about commerce every day, and I'm passionate about helping retailers grow their business. When they succeed, we succeed.

If you liked this book, you've got to check out our website: www.demacmedia.com. In addition to the resources accompanying this book, we've got more than 1,100 articles we've published over the last five years, dealing with every facet of Ecommerce and retail. We're constantly writing and publishing whenever we learn something new. We've got benchmark reports and even some data from our own site showing how we're doing.

Along those lines, if you enjoyed this book, please share it with your retail friends. One of our company's core values is to share everything, which is why we publish so much content. If this book improved your business, I'm confident it can help others you know.

If you're interested in working with us, we make a living helping merchants build and grow their Ecommerce business through design, technology development, optimization, and marketing. We focus on a handful of things that we know can affect profitable, consistent commerce. In effect, we're an outside Ecommerce team for companies that don't have the specialists they need on staff.

I would wish you good luck, but you don't need it. You've got a Commerce Canvas, a personalized roadmap to success. You're ready to stand out in the future of sameness, avoid shiny objects, do the right things at the right time, and dominate commerce for years to come!

ACKNOWLEDGMENTS

It's sort of a weird thing, creating and publishing a book. It's a form of content I've simply never thought I'd put my name on. Having met and spoken with a number of authors over the years, it was no surprise that the endeavor of writing, publishing, and marketing a book would be a ton of work.

Early on in the process I asked some friends who've been down this road for advice. The one resounding theme was to build a great team. It seems obvious now, since creating a book is no different from the rest of my professional career. Building anything takes time, and building anything of significance takes a team. Why would a book be any different?

With that said, this book wouldn't even exist if it weren't for a long list of people who have been a part of my life for the last eight-plus years. Without them, I wouldn't have been able to go through this process and most certainly wouldn't have had the experiences that formed the basis for everything you just read in this book.

Without my loving and always supportive wife, Jen, my amazing team at Demac Media, and our merchant partners that give us the space to be creative problem solvers, this book simply wouldn't exist. Heck, much of my professional self wouldn't be what it is today without this group of people challenging and helping me.

A "thank you" doesn't seem to quite cut it.

ABOUT THE AUTHOR

MATTHEW BERTULLI is CEO and cofounder of Demac Media, a company of marketers, designers, and developers that helps merchants of all sizes grow and optimize their ecommerce businesses. Demac Media helps its merchant partners get hundreds of millions of dollars in online sales every year.

Made in the USA
San Bernardino, CA
06 August 2017